HOW TO ADD HUMOR TO YOUR NOVEL

Learn to Write Funny Scenes

Lisa Wells

Up All Night Publishing

Edited by: The Word Slayers

Cover by: Fan Favorite Digital

www.lisawellsauthor.com

This book is dedicated to Margie Lawson.
You are the teacher behind the success of so many
authors--myself included.
Thank you for being my champion.

Contents

One

WHY DO PEOPLE LAUGH?

WHY DO
PEOPLE
LAUGH

B efore you can add humor to your writing, you need to know what makes a person laugh. If you were to ask Google, "WHAT MAKES A PERSON LAUGH?," you'd discover 428 million helpful(ish) links on the topic.

I clicked on a lot of those links during my research and found they all basically point toward nine inducers of laughter (IOLs). Of those nine, six are useful to a writer. Those six are:

1. Release – We laugh when our emotions get too wound up and we don't know what to do or say; the laughter releases us from that pending storm. This is why people often laugh at inappropriate times. It's not because they're social misfits; it's simply because their emotions need a release valve, and laughing is often seen as a safer outlet than crying.

2. Embarrassment – The next time you do something embarrassing in front of someone else, check: Did you laugh? It's a common reaction when you find yourself in an awkward situation.

3. Recognition – When you hear someone say something that's exactly what you've thought or done but hadn't realized you weren't alone in your weirdness, you laugh. It's a moment of sisterhood or brotherhood or humanhood between you and another person.

4. Incongruity – This kind of laughter occurs when you think someone is going to say one thing, but they say something completely different that still fits in a weird, fun way.

5. Surprise – Good surprises make us laugh. If you're looking for a magic pill to induce laughter in your readers, surprise is it.

6. Superiority – This is when something is said not everyone will get – but because you do, you laugh. It's like you and the speaker/author are

in on a secret together. Pixar movies are full of superiority hits that cause parents to laugh - but not the children, because the little ones don't get it.

Now that you know what induces laughter in a person, the next question becomes: How do you write something that'll create laughter in the reader? I'd like to say this is the easy part, but considering only 1% of laughter is created by the written word, I'd be blowing smoke up your Bluetooth keyboard.

You see, most laughter results from a person both hearing and seeing something he finds laugh-worthy. Body language, tone, and setting are huge when it comes to creating laughter. I tell you this not to discourage you, but to point out while this book will give you a variety of tools to use when striving to induce laughter in your reader, if you don't take out those tools and become very intimate with them, nothing much will change.

Let the familiarity begin.

Two

FINDING YOUR READER'S FUNNY BONE

FINDING YOUR READER'S FUNNY BONE

Y ou—the author—need to know what your readers find funny, which means you need to do some research. Luckily, you live in the age of social media. So, you can simply pop onto Facebook or Instagram or TikTok and ask your readers what they find funny.

Or you can read the bestselling books written by other authors in your genre and see what style of humor they utilize to make their readers laugh.

If their audience is your audience—and their books are flying off the proverbial shelf— then what they do to make their readers laugh will also make your readers laugh.

I've done my research and found a few of the things my readers love are: snark, innuendos, and zingers. They don't like slapstick humor.

Once you know what makes your readers laugh, you can purposefully incorporate those inducers-of-laughter into your books. The second part of that sentence ("you can purposefully incorporate those inducers-of-laughter into your books") is mostly what this book will cover.

So, let's get started.

ASSIGNMENT: What Makes Your Readers Laugh?

Record your answers to the above question in a notebook or computer file.

Three

HUMOR GUIDES

HUMOR GUIDES

I f you want to be able to put funny on the page, you need to find a humor guide. Someone who does what you want to do. Someone you can stalk (shadow) via the written word.

Yes – the written word. Because this is a book for authors who want to learn how to add humor to the page, your guide needs to be an author who writes in your genre. Starting with their most highly rated book, read what they've published.

When your guide does something in a book that makes you laugh, ask yourself how you could use that technique in your manuscript.

Author Darynda Jones is one of my go-to authors to shadow. I also like Janet Evanovich. And Sarah Ballance. And...well, there are many.

ASSIGNMENT: Pick the first chapter of one of your Humor Guide's books, and study it in-depth. Keep a running tally of how many humor hits they have in chapter one. If they average 30 humor hits in the first chapter, then that's your goal with your books. If they have only one or two, then that's your goal. THE NUMBER OF HUMOR HITS WILL VARY BY GENRE. If they have no humor hits in their first chapter, then read the whole book and see how many they have in the book. Some genres may have only a half-dozen.

If you want extra credit, take the above assignment a step further and rate the humor hits. Are they lip-twitchers? Giggle inducers? Or snort-illicit-drugs-out-of-your-nose causers? This extra credit step will let you know what level of humor you need to aim to achieve.

Are your readers wanting LOL reads? Or are they looking for something lower key...yet humorous?

ASSIGNMENT: From now until your visit to the Pearly Gates (or the Gates you imagine seeing in your afterlife), every time you read something that causes you to snort chocolate milk or chardonnay or brain matter out of your nose, PLEASE write it down, analyze it, and understand how the reader pulled it off.

BONUS ASSIGNMENT: Start a new page in your journal, and write down what you see on T-shirts, funny signs, memes, etc., that would make your reader laugh. Repurpose the material for use as dialogue and character thoughts in your novels.

As I mentioned at the start of this section, NYT best-selling author Darynda Jones is one of my go-to authors to shadow. In my opinion, she writes super funny scenes.

Below, I'm sharing with you the first chapter of her book: *It's a Good Day for Chardonnay* (yes, Darynda gave me permission to share the first chapter). The bolded words are humor hints.

Note: What you find funny may be different. That's not the point of this assignment. The point is, this author is adored by readers of the same genres in which I write. Her humor on the page can point me in the direction of what my readers will find funny.

A GOOD DAY FOR CHARDONNAY

Welcome to Del Sol

Home of Something . . .

Or Somebody Famous . . .

Someday . . .

Maybe . . .

Sunshine stared into her cup of coffee as though it were a witch's cauldron, a window revealing all the ways she could kill her parents. Their deaths would be slow and methodical and painful. **Much like the date she was on now.**

She looked across the table at said date—the third one her parents had set her up with in as many weeks—and feigned interest by **lifting a brow in dire need of professional attention.**

"There's a lot more to pest control than people realize."

She'd tried to wax her own brows once.

"Our work can get pretty dangerous."

Ripping out one's facial hair took nerve.

"Last year I was attacked by a swarm of carnivorous beetles."

And painkillers.

"Another time, I thought I'd been bitten by a copperhead and fell down three flights of stairs."

And possibly a blood coagulant.

"Turns out I was just electrocuted."

If Sun were totally honest with herself—

"I will never stick my hand inside an RV's plumbing system again."

—and she liked to think she was—

"I don't care what the literature says."

—Carver wasn't the worst date she'd ever had.

"Then there was the time I tried to tame a jellyfish."

His height alone was enough to turn heads.

"Its name was Loki."

And he'd been graced with thick muddy curls.

"He glowed in the dark."

Ashen-gray eyes.

"Not that Loki had anything to do with my job."

And a sharp angular face.

"It's just, in case you've ever wondered—"

On a scale of one to Ferrari, Carver was a solid Ford Explorer.

"—jellyfish cannot be domesticated."

He'd make some lucky girl a fine ex-husband one day.

"I have the doctor's bills to prove it."

Still, there was something off about him.

"They don't have brains."

Something Sun couldn't quite put her finger on.

"Jellyfish. Not doctors."

He was handsome but not in a charming way.

"Insects do though."

Smart but not in a clever way.

"Did you know there are over five million species of insects in the world?"

Nice but not in a genuine way.

"And thirty-five thousand species of spiders."

In a word, he was not Levi Ravinder.

"Thankfully, they rarely bother humans."

But so few men were.

"Even ones as pretty as you."

True, Carver paled in comparison to Levi, but so did every other man Sun had ever met. The fact that she'd been in love with the guy since she was a kid didn't help. No one stood a chance against the bad boy from a crime-ridden family who'd done good.

And now, instead of being with the man of her dreams, she was stuck with bug guy. **She could only hope her parents'd had the foresight to buy side-by-side burial plots before setting her up.**

"Is that your phone?"

Sunshine snapped out of her musings and dug through her bag for her phone like it was a life preserver on the Titanic. "Hello?" she said, sounding more desperate than she'd intended. She cleared her throat and began again. "Sheriff Vicram."

A male voice eerily resembling her BFF's spoke in hushed tones. "You told me to call if he came back."

Sun froze. Her sidekick since kindergarten, who also happened to be her chief deputy, sounded panicked.

Though he did seem to panic more often than most men, Sun fought a wave of anxiety.

"Randy," he added.

"He didn't."

"Did too," he said defensively.

"Okay, look, stay calm, Quince."

Quincy Cooper had been her bestie since she'd throat-punched Peter Bailey for knocking him down on the playground. Quince had grown since then. Now **he looked roughly like an industrial freezer with a grin** that could melt the panties off a comatose nun.

Peter Bailey eventually got throat cancer but Sun liked to think it had less to do with her throat punch and more to do with his three-pack-a-day habit.

"Stay calm?" he mimicked, incredulous. "You stay calm. Have you seen the size of this guy?"

"Quince, we've got this." She grabbed her bag and stood. "Call for backup. Everyone. Get Zee and Salazar there ay-sap. I'll be there in five. By the way, who's Randy?"

He released an annoyed sigh, drawing it out as though he were competing for Miss Drama Queen USA. "The raccoon."

She stopped, slammed her eyes shut, and spun to face away from her date. When she spoke, she spoke softly so Carver the pest-preneur wouldn't overhear. "You called me about a raccoon?"

"Yes, I called you about a raccoon. You told me to. He's wreaking havoc all over town."

"All over town as in your house."

"There, too."

She took a deep breath and turned back to Carver. "I'm so sorry. I've been called in. Power outages on the other side of town. **People running into walls. It's utter chaos.**"

He shot out of his chair. "Oh, no, that's okay. I mean, you are the sheriff."

There.

That odd niggling at the back of her neck.

It was the way he said sheriff. As though her holding such a position was preposterous. Never mind her master's degree in criminal justice. Or her ten years on the Santa Fe police force seven of which she served as a detective. To him, she was a curvy blonde. End of story. She'd sensed it the moment his gaze landed on her.

And her breasts.

Mostly her breasts.

Curse her ability to read people like the ingredients label on a bottle of water.

Most people, anyway. Levi Ravinder? Not so much.

When she started to walk away, Carver called out to her. "Do you want me to get this?"

She stopped again, stunned. After a moment, she took a deep, calming breath. As slowly and methodically as she'd been planning her parents' deaths, she pivoted around to him. "Not at all." She walked back, took out a ten, and dropped it onto the table.

"Oh, yours was only a couple of bucks."

She knew exactly how much her cup of coffee was. It was a freaking cup of coffee. With a nod, she gestured toward his triple espresso caramel soy macchiato with a dash of cinnamon and extra nondairy whip, and said, "It's on me."

He beamed at her, clearly impressed. "Well, thank you, Sunshine. Most women don't take that kind of initiative."

And she'd moisturized for this.

"I'd love to see you again."

Wedging a smile between the hard lines that had marbleized her face, she turned and headed out the door. Not that she'd actually expected him to pay for her coffee. Going dutch was always best in these situations. But, seriously, it was a dollar fifty.

One.

Dollar.

Fifty.

A buck and a half.

Twelve bits.

She couldn't rush off to her power outage fast enough. The fact that she'd lied about it was entirely beside the point.

She unlocked her cruiser and settled inside, thankful she hadn't dressed so **much to the nines as to the five-and-dimes. Sixes at best**. Sure, she'd applied makeup, a rarity these days, but she wore a peach summery sweater, faded jeans, and pretty suede boots with just enough of a heel to make her a danger to herself and anyone within a ten-foot radius.

Making a quick U-turn out of the parking lot, she headed toward Quince's house. **She almost felt bad about abandoning her half-date soy latte with a splash of objectification and extra nondairy whipped misogyny.** Carver was new in town, the owner and operator of the Four Cs. a.k.a. the Creepy Crawler Critter Control. And he—

Wait. She stepped on the brakes and frowned in thought. How did someone get an RV up three flights of stairs?

Sun had to make the arduous drive through the town of Del Sol to get to Quincy's cabin. So like five minutes. Caffeine-Wah had opened the outdoor area beside their coffee shop. Both locals and tourists sat around a blazing firepit despite the sultry night, listening to an acoustic guitarist and drinking cappuccinos spiked with either Irish cream or Dark River Shine, Del Sol's homegrown corn whiskey.

Even the newlyweds, Ike and Ida Madrid, were there, with their prize rooster, Puff Daddy, on a leash, much to the delight of the other patrons. Four months ago, those two had been mortal enemies, and yet marriage became them. Surely there was hope for the rest of humanity. And Sun. Eventually.

She glanced over at a couple of the locals as she passed, only mildly curious where one might obtain a leash for a rooster. Bernadette, the owner of Swirls-N-Curls, and Juana the owner of Sun's favorite Mexican restaurant, Tia Juana's, sat at a high table having way too much fun for there to only be coffee in their cups.

The two women were Del Sol natives, born and raised, thus Sun's mind meandered to the question that had been plaguing her since moving back. She'd been encouraged—a.k.a. blackmailed—into looking into a local myth that had been around for decades, about the Dangerous Daughters a group of women, who according to legend, secretly ran the town.

Because of that, she looked at every woman who'd been born and raised in the small hamlet as a potential Daughter. But she just couldn't see Bernadette running a town. A bingo parlor maybe, or a speakeasy, but not a town.

Juana, however, was another story. That woman could run a battalion.

Sun took a right at the town square and spotted Doug, their local flasher, walking toward the illuminated park. Painfully thin and wearing his usual trench coat, thick glasses, and a headband with a feather in it, he made a U-turn when he saw her cruiser and headed down a dark alley. She'd clearly foiled his plans for the evening. Served him right. That man was a menace.

Feeling good about the fact that she'd saved an innocent pedestrian from a flashing that could never be unseen, Sun drove out to Del Sol Lake and parked down the street from Quincy's cabin. Mostly because she had no choice. He'd taken her quite literally when she said to call in everyone.

Two deputy's vehicles sat on one side of the narrow road leading to his house along with several vehicles whose owners Sun could only speculate. Though one did look hauntingly familiar. White Buick Encore. Cracked taillight. Sign that read Honk if you like the taco. **Which did not mean what her mother thought it meant.**

Sun spared a moment to pinch the bridge of her nose when a hand shot out of a bush and pulled her behind it. Thankfully the hand was attached to a body. A body named Quincy Lynn Cooper.

Wearing a pair of night-vision goggles that covered the upper half of his face, he dragged her around the cabin and yanked her behind yet another bush, before shushing her with an index finger over his mouth and pointing to his back porch.

"I didn't say anything," she whispered, slapping at his hand, annoyed at being yanked while having to navigate the rough terrain in heels.

"He's there," Quince said, his whisper much softer than hers. It was then that Sun realized he was wearing full tactical gear to go with the goggles and comm set. It took everything in her not to react, and she fought a strong urge to pinch the bridge of her nose again.

Instead, she looked through the foliage and saw nothing. "Where?"

"There." He pointed toward the shadows of his back porch. "Somewhere. I heard him, but the coward is too afraid to show his face when I'm around."

Sun frowned. Stakeouts were not a favorite pastime, and who knew how long it would be before the masked bandit emerged from the home he'd invaded. The same home he'd been invading repeatedly for weeks, according to the behemoth beside her.

Quincy's small cabin sat on the banks of the Pecos River, and she let the sound of rushing water wash over her. She could even smell it. Fresh and clear. His cabin had previously been a rental for tourists and resembled four others just like it, but they were far enough apart to offer a nice bit of privacy thanks to some strategically placed vegetation.

Maroon paint, in bad need of a fresh coat, framed the exposed pine exterior and wraparound porch that ran the length of the abode. Sun loved little more than sitting on that porch with Quincy, sipping on a glass of chardonnay and watching the setting sun glisten over the Pecos like diamonds and ambers and amethysts. But the sun had set an hour earlier, hence the goggles.

When he handed her a pair along with a comm set and a quick, "Here" Sun fought a giggle. He'd gone all out. For a raccoon. She took the equipment and feigned a fit of coughs to cover her amusement.

He didn't buy it. He pressed his mouth together and ignored her as she struggled to untangle a blond lock of hair from a branch then slipped the headset onto her head.

"Quince," she said, letting her eyes adjust to the green glow behind the goggles to focus on figure after figure stalking through the forested area, "when I said to call everyone in, I didn't mean, you know, *everyone*."

"Well then, you shouldn't have said everyone. Besides, I needed help from on high."

"God?" she asked, fitting the earpiece he handed her into her left ear.

"No, sniper. Zee is on top of Mr. Chavez's barn."

A hushed female voice came over the radio. "You look great, boss."

Then another. Deputy Tricia Salazar, a curvy twenty-something with doe eyes and chipmunk cheeks, was learning to be Zee's spotter. "I agree. You should wear your civvies more often, boss."

Sun turned and, even though she couldn't actually see the deputies atop the rickety barn, flashed them her best supermodel smile. She could only imagine what that looked like with the alien tactical gear on her face.

"Thank you, guys." She tossed her hair over a shoulder. "At least someone noticed."

"Oh yeah," Quincy said, keeping a weather eye on his back porch. "How'd the date go?"

"**Well enough to justify a plea of temporary insanity when I kill my parents.** Why are you risking my deputies' lives for a rodent?"

He snorted. "They'll be fine. Even if they fall, it's not a tall barn. They'll shake it off."

"Like when you fell off your grandfather's barn and cried for two hours?"

"I was six. What did this one do for a living?"

"You mean after my last blind date, **the breatharian life coach?**"

"Yeah." He scratched his chin. "I wouldn't have figured your mother as one to set you up with a man living out of his van. **Clearly, you're depreciating with age.**"

"Clearly. Mom said he was still finding himself."

"How old was he?"

"Early seventies. Thankfully, tonight's victim was more age-appropriate. And he had a job! Pest control. Or at least I think it was pest control. I wasn't really paying attention." When he ripped off the goggles and turned to gape at her, his eyes glowing green through her lenses, she asked, "What?"

"Let me get this straight," he said, ironically straightening to his full height of six feet, four inches, with shoulders spanning a similar distance. "You were on a date with a pest control guy when I called with a pest control issue, and you left him at the café?"

She stabbed him with **the best glare in her arsenal, number 12.2—she'd recently upgraded**—even

though its genius was wasted behind the goggles.
"Of course I left him at the café. Can you imagine what he would've charged for an after-hours emergency?"

"Budget issues?"

She snorted. "That's an understatement. My left pinky is bigger than our budget."

He gave her a surprised once-over. "As opposed to your right one?"

"I know right? I have weird fingers."

"Please. You should see my toes."

"I want to see them," Zee said over the comm.

"Never, sis. My toes are very private."

Quincy and Zee had decided they were twins separated at birth when they met four months ago. Since Quince was a blond-haired, blue-eyed wreck with few worthwhile talents—because the ability to sleep standing up didn't count—and Zee was a tall, gorgeous black woman who could shoot the wings off a fruit fly at hundred yards, Sun highly doubted the validity of their claim. Also, neither was adopted. So there was that.

"Okay, Quince, I have a random, off-the-cuff question," **Sun said randomly and off-the-cuff.**

"Shoot."

"What in the name of God is my mother doing here?" Sun watched as her mother tiptoed through the sultry night air, easing closer to Quincy's back porch. She'd pulled her graying blond hair into a ponytail that always made her look younger than her fifty-five years. A gauze tunic hung loosely over her slim frame.

"You said to call for backup."

"And you called my mother?" she asked, her voice rising a notch.

"No. I called her book club. Those ladies are fierce." The grin he wore made it impossible to be annoyed. He had a point, after all.

Sun scanned the area, now littered with women who'd run out of fucks to give decades ago, and focused on two in particular. **They carried butterfly nets, one as though it were an assault rifle, the other as though it were a missile launcher.**

"Just two more quick questions," she said.

He pulled the goggles back into position, and said, "Hit me."

"Why the hell do they have butterfly nets and where did they get them on such short notice?"

He chuckled and gestured toward a wily, five-foot firecracker in full camouflage regalia and neon pink crocs that were so blinding through the goggles Sun had to look away. Wanda also happened to be the one carrying her butterfly net like a missile launcher which fit her personality to a tee.

"I think every time the men in white coats come for Wanda, she steals their nets and runs away."

The deputies laughed softly through the comm, Zee's an alluring, husky thing, and Deputy Salazar's a bubbly giggle like champagne. **Or denture-cleaning tablets.**

"That wouldn't surprise me," Sun said wondering in the back of her mind if any of her mother's book club mates could be associated with the Dangerous Daughters. If it were even real. "It would also not surprise me if she brought the butterfly net more for you than for the raccoon."

He laughed again, but quickly changed his mind. Concern flashed across the part of his boyishly handsome face that she could see. "You're joking, right?"

Sun shrugged. Wanda had always had a thing for the intrepid deputy. Sadly, the intrepid deputy had always had a thing for Sun's mother, which would explain his calling in her book club more than his lame-ass excuse.

She used to think Quincy's crush was just a post-pubescent schoolboy thing, but since she'd moved back to Del Sol four months ago, Quince constantly asked about her mom, the lovely Elaine Freyr. How was she? What she was up to? Had she ever had an affair with a younger, freakishly comely man?

It was weird. And getting weirder every day. So much so, in fact, that Sun had caught onto his ruse about a month in. He was deflecting. Straight up. He was in love with someone else, and he didn't want her to know. Her. Sunshine Vicram. His best friend since the sandbox.

Sun vowed to find out who he was rounding the bases and sliding into home with if it were the last thing she did on this Earth. **To date, she'd narrowed it down to thirty-seven women (and two men just in case). She was so close she could taste victory. Or wishful thinking. Emotional figures of speech tasted startlingly similar.**

Her phone dinged with a text from her date asking if everything was okay.

Before she could answer, Quincy whispered so loudly he probably scared off the masked bandit. "There he is!"

Sun glanced at the porch and, sure enough, the little guy was climbing out of a tiny hole in the ceiling of Quincy's porch as though being poured out of it, his fur fluffing up to three times his actual size. **It reminded Sun she needed to cut back on the carbs.**

Quince slid his goggles down and raised his dart gun, a non-lethal tranquilizer launcher that looked like a combination of an Uzi and a water gun.

"Please don't tranq my mother," Sun said, cringing as she stood beside him and watched the critter through her goggles.

Before he could get a clear shot, however, Wanda ran forward, her net at the ready. "I'll get 'em!"

"Shit," Quince said. Abandoning his cover, he vaulted around the bush toward the melee of vigilant women.

Sun fought off the branch again and followed, trying not to twist her ankle. She watched as Wanda, her mother, and Darlene Tapia, another member of the infamous Book Babes Book Club, ascended the stairs to the porch and rushed the panicked, screeching creature.

Poor little guy. Sun would've screeched, too. Those women were alarmingly fast runners.

"Don't get near it!" Quincy shouted.

"It's okay, handsome." Wanda took a swipe at the ball of fur, just missing it by several tenths of a mile. "I was vaccinated for rabies when I was a kid. I'm immune."

Sun's heart jumped into her throat as Wanda got closer. The rabies angle had yet to occur to her. "I'm not sure it works that way, Wanda!"

"I can't see anything," Elaine Freyr said, now watching from a safe-ish distance on the porch as her friends advanced. She spun in a complete circle, searching the shadows of the porch. "Where'd it go?"

Darlene Tapia followed suit. All three women were in the dizzying midst of full-on adrenaline rushes, screaming and recoiling with the slightest movement, Wanda swinging wildly as the raccoon scurried about trying to escape. Wanda was either going to kill the raccoon or concuss someone else.

Quincy took up position about ten feet out and raised the rifle again.

"Don't you dare," Sun said, glaring at him as she ran past. She hiked up the stairs, ducked another swipe from Wanda's net, and slid to a stop beside her mother, her gaze darting about.

"Son of a bitch," Quincy said with more whine than all of southern France. "He got away."

"And whose fault would that be?" she asked him over her shoulder. She turned back to the maniac who'd birthed her. "Mom, it's okay. We've got this." When Elaine didn't move, Sun put a hand on her arm. "Mom?"

Her mother stood frozen, staring up into a darkened corner of the porch. Sun pivoted slowly and came face-to-face with a very angry raccoon, their noses only inches apart.

It sat hunchbacked on a high windowsill, a slow hiss leaking from between its exposed teeth, as it gazed at her with wide, feral eyes. Eyes that glowed like they belonged to a creature possessed by a powerful evil. One so ancient, so primordial, it predated human language.

Then she realized she was still wearing the goggles and the ominous metaphor lost its ardor. Much like Sun's hopes to go her entire life without wrestling a raccoon in the dark with a gang of bookworms cheering her on. But stranger things had happened.

Before she could react, she heard the thud of compressed air. Quincy had taken a shot with her barely inches from the terrified animal. What the actual hell?

He'd just moved up a notch on her hit list, overtaking Ryan Spalding, a boy who'd claimed she'd given him a hand job under the bleachers in high school, when she realized it was a misfire. The gun. Not the hand job. She'd never touched Ryan's penis much to his chagrin.

Quincy let loose a dozen expletives followed by a sheepishly meek, "Misfire."

She wanted to roll her eyes but didn't dare take them off the rodent. They were locked in a stare-down of legendary proportions. "Zee," she said softly into her comm set, staying as still as she possibly could, "you wanna help me out here?"

Zee's smooth voice came back to her. "Will do, boss." Her calm tone spoke volumes. Like elevator music. **Or an acid trip.** She was already in the zone and probably had the creature in her crosshairs. "One inch to the left."

Sun eased to her left a microsecond before a dart whizzed past her ear.

It hit home just as the raccoon catapulted off the sill and **onto her goggle-covered face.** She screamed and sank her fingers in its fur to rip it off, but it held on for dear life, anchoring its razor-sharp claws in her scalp. She stumbled back and tripped on something hard and short. **Probably her own indignation.**

Her mother screamed but it barely registered before Sun found herself falling. No. Not just falling. Tumbling, suddenly weightless. She'd done a backflip over the wooden porch railing and seemed to be plummeting headfirst toward certain death.

A familiar set of arms caught her in mid-air before all three—the owner of said arms, the facehugger, and Sun herself—slammed onto the rocky earth beneath them. Air whooshed out of her lungs, and, even with the insulation of her rescuer, the hard landing sent a jolt of pain through body parts that, until that moment, she was unaware existed.

It also dislodged the raccoon. The furball shot into the darkness and landed a few feet away with a soft thud.

She rolled off her rescuer and lay on her back, gazing up at the stars and gasping to force air into lungs that had seized up, when her mother's head popped into her line of sight.

"Honey, are you okay?" she asked, concern lining her pretty, upside-down face.

"Peachy, Mom" Sun said, her voice strained. **"Thanks for asking."** Her gaze slid past the woman who birthed her and back up to the stars again, hoping for a glimpse of the Little Dipper, wishing she could pluck it from the heavens and beat her chief deputy with it. "Deputy Cooper?"

"Yeah, boss?" he replied, panting close by.

"Are you conscious?"

"Yes."

"Can you give me one good reason why I shouldn't beat you to death with a feather duster?"

"I made you bacon the other day."

Damn it.

According to my calculations, there are 37 humor hits in the first chapter of *It's a Good Day for Chardon-*

nay. That's a lot of humor hits. When I analyzed how funny they were, I found they all fell within the range of lip twitchers and giggle inducers. She used a lot of techniques you'll learn about throughout this book. Techniques like simple truths, comedic characters, and cliché twists.

This might be a good time to mention Darynda Jones was in the first group of students who took my month-long humor class at Lawson's Writers Academy. While she was freaking-funny long before she took my class, she now utilizes the tools I'm sharing with you in this book to enhance how she puts humor on the page.

ASSIGNMENT: After you've read the first chapter of a book written by your chosen Humor Guide, take the time to reflect upon their techniques. Then brainstorm on how you can incorporate one of their techniques into one of your books. DON'T steal. Make it your own.

For example: In the opening scene of Darynda's book, she has two characters involved in a dialogue tangent. *A dialogue tangent is where two characters are in a conversation but both fixated on separate topics.*

Darynda has her scene masterfully set up where one character is talking and the other is responding (completely off-topic) internally. I teach this technique in my dialogue class and have used it in my own books, but Darynda's example of the technique is masterful. By studying her opening chapter, I'm reminded of all the fun I can have with dialogue techniques. Fun that can create laughter in my readers.

Four

WHAT MAKES YOU LAUGH?

LAUGHTER

WHAT
MAKES YOU
LAUGH

H opefully, your sense of humor somewhat meshes with your readership. That kind of meshing will make your life easier. Trust me, if you write for middle schoolers (or teach or counsel them), it helps to have a warped sense of humor.

Why do I want you to track what makes you laugh? Easy. Things that make you laugh are fodder for what you can tweak and then place in your future books to make your readers laugh.

ASSIGNMENT: Create a laughter file and add at least three things a week to this file. Don't be lazy. Do this assignment. You'll thank me later.

Here are some things that recently made me laugh.

1. A T-shirt that read: "Beer - It's not just for breakfast anymore."

2. A collision repair shop ad sponsored by the rabbit who's really glad you hit the power pole instead of him.

3. A radio station that played the audio of a woman blasting the whole morning crew for being idiots and on drugs and how she'd never listen to them - even if they were the last radio station on Earth. AND then, instead of responding to the audio complaint, the radio station went right to a song. They viewed her blasting of them as an endorsement – and that made me laugh.

Someday, a variation of the T-shirt quote will come out of the mouth of one of my characters. For instance, if I had a character who leaned toward the tell-it-like-you-see-it-side, she might, in reference to the commercialization of Christmas, say something snarky like, "Christmas – it's not just for Christians anymore."

Or if I was writing an enemies-to-lovers book, one of my characters might say, "Revenge...it's not just for Rambo anymore."

By having a mentor, I learned to notice the sayings on T-shirts and thus came upon one I could twist and use to put funny on the page of a future novel.

*If you have children in your books, follow teachers on TikTok. They share the funny things their students say and do. **Tip: Don't just listen to teachers of TikTok, write down what they're sharing about**

what their students say and do. You can then repurpose/tweak one of those moments into a funny scene in one of your novels.

One of my favorite accounts is "@gregisms #storytime." Here are three things from his account that are written in my folder of things that made me laugh and how I could repurpose them into future books:

1. "Don't be a butt sandwich." 1st grader tattling on another student (in a novel, you could easily have a child say this to a parent who is being a *butt sandwich* to a potential love interest, and it could be a source of humor for a scene you're writing).

2. "Bye, Gay." A kindergartener-little girl said this to Mr. Greg—after he'd dropped by her class to introduce himself at the beginning of the school year. The comment was made in a friendly tone as he left. Obviously, the child has a developed gaydar (blurting out observations that might offend the listener would be a cute personality trait to have in a child in a future book. I once sat next to a little girl at a repair shop who asked the Black man sitting next to her why his palms weren't black).

3. A 5th grader looked Mr. Greg up and down, pointed to what he was wearing, and said, "This is busted." *Note – I don't know if "busted" is good or bad, but I can still use this in dialogue in a book. And so could you.

@Gregisms concerning life in general

1. "I Di-Greg" (Mr. Greg says this when he's gone off subject). I could have a character with that speech quirk.

2. This Christmas, Mr. Greg put out a lot of tacky Christmas lights and yard signs with a sign that says, "We good Peggy?" (Peggy is his neighbor, who was "disap-

pointed" in his Halloween decorations) Bits of this could easily be repurposed into a scene in one of my books.

3. Greg to an Uber driver, "Do you like driving an Uber?" The driver replied, "It was either this or working the streets. And I got more customers with this" (the personality of an upbeat Uber driver who likes to chat could be something funny to add in a book someplace).

*If your readers are like mine and like snark, innuendo, and zingers, I also suggest following accounts like Fuckology on Instagram. Tidbits of its daily posts are often added to my what-made-me-laugh file, which I peruse when pondering the perfect zinger for one of my characters to mouth off. Remember: My readers like zingers.

Here are three items from Fuckology that are now in my made-me-laugh file, and notes on how to use them in future novels.

1. My five-year plan is to make it through this year (could be used in a job interview scene).

2. Why do people talk before 9 in the morning? Shut the fuck up (could be the thoughts of a character).

3. I solve all my problems by creating 3 new ones as distractions (could be a funny character quirk - how that character resolves problems in her life).

Five

HOW TO FUNNY-UP YOUR CHARACTERS

HOW TO FUNNY-UP YOUR CHARAC-TERS

A s a fiction author, you know the importance of carefully choosing your story's characters. If your desire is to add more humor to your writing, then when choosing your characters, you need to think in terms of how they can help you in your funny quest.

Remember when I mentioned one of the things Darynda did to add humor in her first chapter was use comedic characters? This chapter will give you the tools to do the same thing.

When comedians are writing their sets, they make use of comedic characters. A comedic character is two-dimensional, with a couple of in-your-face traits. Their lack of dimension is what makes them funny. But when authors write their books, they create dramatic (multi-dimensional) characters. This doesn't mean we can't draw from the character-development toolbox of comedians. We most certainly can.

In any given scene in our books, we can focus tightly on just one or two of the traits of one of our beloved/not beloved characters. The traits you hyper-focus on will no longer be ordinary traits. They'll become obsessive traits that are triggered in a scene.

One of the things that might trigger your characters' traits into obsessions would be the settings they find themselves in. Settings they aren't used to. Let me explain.

When comedians and creators of sitcoms create their characters, they may choose to place a normal character in an abnormal setting or an abnormal character in a normal setting. Why? Because those combinations make people laugh. *In other words, they use a fish-out-of-water trope that bends toward the funny side.

Think about your favorite sitcoms. What combination do the writers use? One of my favorites to watch right now is *United States Of Al*. In this sitcom, the main character, Al, is from Afghanistan. He's now living with the American family of one of the soldiers he worked for as a translator. Al, who's from Afghanistan, is an abnormal character placed in what the viewers think of as a normal setting: Everyday life in America. His supporting cast members are all normal (American born) characters. The differences in their upbringings and beliefs make for a lot of humor. In a few of this season's shows, the writers generated laughs by playing up the differences in how Americans search out love and marriage versus how it's done in Afghanistan.

We can do this as authors as well. The next time you're plotting a book, tag your main characters as normal or abnormal. From there, you'll know what types of supporting characters to surround them with, and what type of setting to drop them into for laughter.

If you think back to Darynda's first chapter, she plopped her normal character (the heroine of the series) into a boring setting (a date with a bug man). This setting triggered the heroine's obsessive/comedic thoughts on how to get even with her parents for their interference in both her professional and love life.

Note: Your character can play a normal role in one scene and abnormal one in another. Confused? Think about *The Big Bang Theory*. Most people would consider Penny the normal one in the cast of that show. But in a lot of the episodes, she's the abnormal one (average IQ) among the brainiacs. Her lack of understanding of what they're talking about often results in laughter. But then you place her in her apartment, hosting a game day football party, and add in her brainiac boyfriend

Leonard, and suddenly she's the normal one, and he's the abnormal one.

So, how do you create characters who can be normal in one scene and abnormal in another? The answer lies in the traits you give them. Those traits we talked about at the beginning of the section.

When you're planning your characters, give them their motivations, quirks, weaknesses, etc. - AND THEN when you want to create a funny scene, EXAGGERATE their motivations or quirks or weaknesses.

For example, in the *Big Bang* scene I mentioned above, Leonard is motivated to impress Penny and fit into her crowd. When she invites him to hang out at her Sunday afternoon football-watching party, this motivation to impress her is exaggerated. Before going, he—who knows nothing about sports—learns EVERY-THING about football, then spouts off what he's learned (in a very textbookish way) during the game. This is an example of a character's motivation being exaggerated to create comedy in a scene.

In Darynda's first chapter, she exaggerates the heroine's desire to get even with her parents by having her comedically plot their demise, all while her boring date drones on about his exaggerated passion for his job.

Here's another example of this technique being used in *The Big Bang Theory*.

Sheldon Cooper: He's an annoying character you can't help tolerating because he's clueless when it comes to social skills, and thus you can't blame him when he doesn't act appropriately. Let's dive into his character. If you've watched the show, I'm certain you can list his personality *stuff* off the top of your head. I know I can. But here they are in a nice list.

Genius I. Q.	**Sheldon's Personality Stuff**		Obsessive Compulsive Disorder
Sarcasm Challenged	**Big Ego**	Fails to feel guilt	Must always be the smartest	Socially clumsy

The creator of the show turns Sheldon's stuff into funny by placing him in scenes where his stuff is EXAGGERATED and thus plays off as obsessions.

Obvious Tip: This is what you'll do in your novel for one or more scenes if you want to add humor to your writing.

Example:

In the beginning – Sheldon and Leonard go into Penny's apartment to deliver a couch while she's at work. Penny's apartment is in total disarray. This disarray is (of course) exaggerated.

Sheldon's obsessive-compulsive cleanliness trait is triggered. Leonard won't allow him to act upon it, but Sheldon can't let go of the thought of the apartment next door being so messy. So, he returns to Penny's apartment in the middle of the night and cleans it, while Penny sleeps.

It's important to note the writer not only exaggerated Sheldon's need to clean, he also exaggerated the setting in which he cleans it. Sheldon's actions were done in the middle of the night, while Penny slept. The scene wouldn't have been nearly as funny had he just snuck over to her apartment once Leonard was gone for the day and cleaned.

In the Sheldon scene, the writers exaggerated four things: The setup scene; the payoff scene; Sheldon's need for cleanliness; and Penny's messiness.

*Keep that in mind when you're adding humor to your story. Look for places you can EXAGGERATE and thus make funnier. I keep capitalizing exaggeration because it's this step that takes a character's stuff and blows it up so much, it no longer resembles your reader's perspective. It's the fact that it's so different from your reader's perspective that makes it funny.

Some of you might be thinking, *This is fine for sitcoms, but how can I make this tool work in my book?*

Go back to Darynda's first chapter and read it again. You'll find the whole thing is exaggerated. Beginning with her date and ending with the whole town trying to catch a raccoon.

Here's another example: From a pretend book, I'm pretending to plot. The current title of this pretend book: *The Trouble With Age.*

Premise: When a top-selling marketing executive of luxury items gets reassigned to work in the company's sister office that markets affordable beauty products aimed at women in their twenties, the marketing executive lies about her age to her new 28-year-old man-child boss, who's declared every day casual Friday.

What could happen if you placed an older woman—obsessed with youth and job-performance perfectionism—in a female-dominated workplace run by a man-child? (I'm assigning her as the normal character placed in an abnormal setting.

Which means I'll exaggerate everything going on in the sister office. For example: A man-child boss will be unconcerned with his employees meeting work deadlines, etc. He often parties with all of them.)

Note: This is where you brainstorm. Here's my brainstorming list.

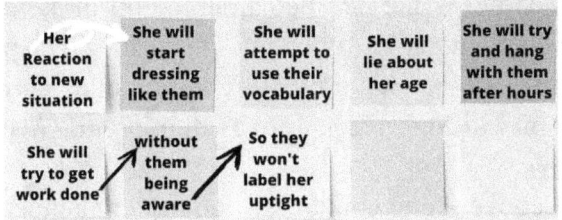

Your question, as a brilliant author, is to ask yourself how you can exaggerate one of those sticky note items and turn it into a comedy scene in your book.

For the purpose of illustration, I chose number three (she'll lie about her age) as our starting point.

Her obsession with youth causes her to lie about her age to all her new co-workers. Not wanting to get caught in this lie, she then decides to obtain a new birth certificate and driver's license as proof of her new fake age (EXAGGERATION AT PLAY).

To make this happen, she travels to the seedier side of town to a location (EXAGGERATE LOCATION) she learned about via the dark(ish) web. There, on a Friday night, she waits outside a bar until a guy is turned away for having a fake ID. She approaches this guy and asks him how to procure one for herself. Tip: The fake ID character is a prime opportunity to add humor to your novel. Don't make him ordinary. Make him funny. EXAGGERATE him.

Later, during the process of obtaining new documentation, our youth-obsessed character ends up in the middle of a sting operation. The leader of the sting operation is a bumbling authority character. *More on bumbling authority characters will come later.

The character selling the fake ID items blames her for the sting. While he's being hauled off in handcuffs, the bad guy threatens to kill my age-obsessed character as soon as he gets out on bail. The bumbling authority insists on whisking her away to a safehouse (EXAGGERATION).

The above scene could easily be used in a meet-cute for a reverse age-gap romantic comedy. In fact, I just might really write it someday. By playing with a character's obsessions and planning a scene to emphasize one of them, I not only came up with a funny scene, I also came up with a future book idea.

Because I think it's important you grasp how vital this step is when it comes to adding humor to your writing, I'm providing you with the obsessions/preoccupations of some famous comedic characters. I'm not telling you who they are. That's not the point. The point is, these characters (with these exaggerated traits) are the basis for some wonderfully funny characters.

CHARACTER ONE	CHARACTER TWO	CHARACTER THREE	CHARACTER FOUR	CHARACTER FIVE
Clean Queen	Bitter	Geek	Trickster	Wary
Bossy pants	Miserly	Socially inept	Master of self-promotion	Unpredictable
Organizational	Selfish	Stress eater	Dubious morality	Spontaneous
wizard	Greedy		Lover of rum	Reckless
Competitive	Dishonest			Loyal

ASSIGNMENT: Now that you have some traits with which to work, pick five of them that could pertain to a character in a book you're writing.

ASSIGNMENT: Pulling from the assignment above, complete a what-could-happen list based on your character's obsession. Example below.

- What could happen if an obsessive CLEAN QUEEN...is a nanny for the children of an artist who allows his children to explore their creativity untethered?
- What could happen if a person who is truly obsessed (think Jack Nicholson in As Good As It Gets) with the spinach soufflé made at the local diner...discovers the chef took the dish off the menu because his heart was broken by the woman who'd inspired the dish?
- What could happen if a wizard of organizing via colors (like the home edit show) gets a new boss who is color blind and insists everything be alphabetically organized?
- What could happen if a woman obsessed with wearing sweaters...is transferred to the Caribbean office?

ASSIGNMENT: Once you've done at least one *what if* (ideally, you'd do at least ten, then choose the best option), go ahead and create the barebones of a scene where that *what if* could blossom into a funny moment in your future book. Remember my example about the older woman who'd been dropped into a young workforce environment? That's what I want you to do.

*Note: I'll be the first to admit my examples above aren't stellar. This is why it's important to do a lot of brainstorming before choosing your best idea. I bet if I'd kept going until I had ten ideas, they would have gotten a lot better. *Lazy brainstorming is not your friend if you want to add excellent hints of humor to your novel.*

Because our choice of characters and the stuff we assign to them will be our NUMBER ONE way to add humor to our books, I'm giving you yet another chart below to help you find a way to come up with ideas that could lead to funny scenes in your books. It's a chart of characters. Your job is to give them something to obsess over. I've filled out a few obsession ideas to get you started.

ASSIGNMENT: COMPLETE this chart.

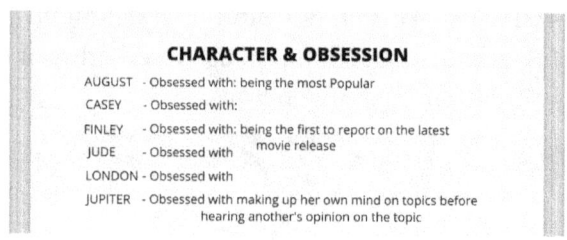

CHARACTER & OBSESSION

AUGUST   - Obsessed with: being the most Popular

CASEY   - Obsessed with:

FINLEY   - Obsessed with: being the first to report on the latest movie release

JUDE   - Obsessed with

LONDON - Obsessed with

JUPITER - Obsessed with making up her own mind on topics before hearing another's opinion on the topic

ASSIGNMENT: Based on the characters on the list – place two of them in a fixed proximity environment (like an elevator or office or bed). Based on their obsessions, how would they react to one another? Put three of them together, how would they interact?

Example: Let's say Jupiter works at a marketing firm and is obsessed with making up her own mind about things. As such, she doesn't want to hear the opinions of others until after she's made up her mind on the topic.

Finley works at the same marketing firm. Finley loves to go to movies on their opening day, then report on them to anyone who'll listen. He considers himself an amateur movie critic.

Unfortunately for Jupiter, the copy machine is right outside of her cubicle, and that's where everyone gathers to gossip.

What happens when you have someone who likes to make up her own mind in close proximity to someone who likes to give his opinion to anyone who'll listen? What are some funny scenes you can think of for these two characters?

Here's my brainstorm of 7 options. I left the last three for you to fill in with your own thoughts on how it could all go down. Remember, anytime we're brainstorming, we want to strive for ten possibilities.

1. Will Jupiter sabotage the copy machine?

2. Will Jupiter file a grievance that says she's suffering mental abuse because others are trying to make up her mind for her? Her grievance will result in being called into human resources for a conversation.

3. Or will she first ask Finley to stop reviewing movies while making copies?

4. What does Finley say when he's asked to stop spouting his thoughts on movies?

5. Does he agree to stop if, in return, Jupiter does something for him?

6. What could that something be (make it funny)? Perhaps it's that Jupiter must pretend to be Finley's girlfriend over the holidays.

7. What if Jupiter says yes to Finley's proposal? But when she gets to the first holiday family gathering, Jupiter is bombarded with a whole family who takes pride in expressing their opinion over dinner? This is Jupiter's worst nightmare. She texts an SOS to HR while sitting there.

8.

9.

10.

Now let's add another character to the above mix. August is obsessed with being the most popular one in any group. How's he going to interact with those at the copy machine who are gossiping?

This one, YOU get to brainstorm.

1.

2.

3.

4.

5.

Remember the tiny note previously saying I'd tell you more about the Bumbling Authority character? Here's that information.

Looking for a shortcut to creating dramatic characters **using comedic characters as your starting point?** This list of comedic character archetypes is for you.

1. The Dummy (Roland Schitt in *Schitt's Creek*)

2. The Slob (Captain Jack Sparrow in *Pirates of the Caribbean*)

3. The Know It All (Sheldon Cooper in *The Big Bang Theory*)

4. The Everyman/Woman (Elaine in *Seinfeld*)

5. Man-child (Howard Walowitz in *The Big Bang Theory*)

6. Klutz (Grace in *Will and Grace*)

7. Lothario (Sam Malone in *Cheers*)

8. Nerd (Chidi in *The Good Place*)

9. Robot/straight woman/man (Grace in *Grace and Frankie*)

10. Naïf (Buddy in *Elf*)

11. Bumbling authority (Inspector Gadget)

12.

Trickster (Chandler in *Friends*)

Writers of sitcoms lean heavily upon what they call the FAB FIVE: The Everyman; the Wisecracker; the Bully; the Dork; the Goofball.

They make these five characters funnier by the use of exaggerations. Everything about the characters is fair game to be exaggerated—their thoughts, their actions, their reactions.

ASSIGNMENT: Watch your favorite sitcoms and, in the table below, make a list of each character's traits. Draw upon these traits when you're creating your own characters.

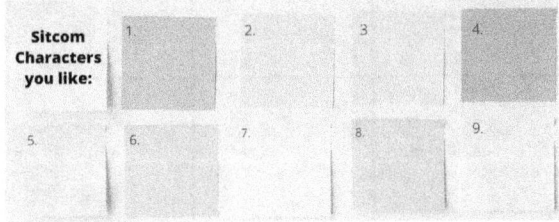

Sitcom Characters you like:	1.	2.	3	4.
5.	6.	7.	8.	9.

Note: I know you know this, but I'm going to say it anyway. While giving your characters all the fun traits you can then blow up, remember also to give them traits that make them lovable. Your novel characters aren't true comedic characters. They're dramatic characters. You're simply giving them *stuff* that can be triggered in certain scenes as a way of adding humor to your novels. Here's a link you can go to to find a huge list of character traits. I've gone through it, and under each of the comedic character types, I've listed what I imagine would be some of their traits.

ASSIGNMENT:

Your job is to peruse the list of traits and pull out some additional traits you can turn into obsessions for comedic purposes during a scene in your novel. On the next couple of pages, I've done a few to get you started.

CHARACTER TYPE	RANDOM TRAITS	RANDOM QUIRKS
Robot Anti-social Calm Boring Unsympathetic stern humorless self-disciplined		
KNOW IT ALL aggressive boisterous bragging blunt gossipy vain smug		
SLOB careless lazy inattentive neglectful friendly scatter-brained		
LOVABLE LOSER/KLUTZ Bashful Clumsy Neurotic Overconfident Rash Talkative Unlucky Unsophisticated romantic	1. reads horoscope daily 2. flirts with old ladies 3.	

CHARACTER TYPE	RANDOM TRAITS	RANDOM QUIRKS
EVERY MAN/WOMAN accommodating authentic average decent wholesome mature ordinary	1. Faints at the sight of blood 2. rearranges things when anxious 3. prone to muttering	1. tinkers with things when stressed 2. sniffs when bored
MAN CHILD/NAIF Entertaining eccentric enthusiastic foolhardy witty naïve	1. fascinated with history 2. interested in UFO's 3. Loves potato chips	1. plays board games against himself 2. interested in royalty
SNOB articulate intolerant narrow-minded reserved poised opinionated offensive		
BUMBLING AUTHORITY incompetent inexperienced insecure misfit kind-hearted loyal gullible		
Trickster Cunning Disruptive Mocks authority mischief fun-loving adventurous amusing impulsive		

Six

CHARACTER MANIFESTOS

*CHARACTER
MANIFESTOS*

O nce you have your lists of character stuff, the next thing I suggest you do is create a manifesto for your main characters. This is not the same as creating a character backstory.

A manifesto is what your character stands for/believes in/embraces joyfully/rejects completely.

When you make this a step in your story plotting, you have a bonus resource for adding humor to your writing. A resource from which to draw when purposefully adding humor to your novel.

A good place to get a feel for what a manifesto is, is to look at ones created by companies. If you Google

"Manifestos," you'll get a large variety to peruse. This is a fun link that'll take you to a manifesto that humorously teaches you how to write a manifesto: https://www.pinterest.com/pin/63402307245658803/ I used it when creating a character manifesto, which I'll share below.

But first, here are a few company manifestos for you to read, to get a feel for what one can be.

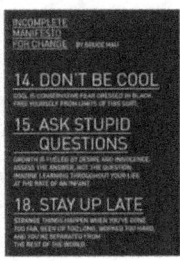

When creating your character manifestos, think about who your characters are at their core. What do they see as the meaning of life? Why is their career important? What are their goals? What are their frustrations? What legacy do they want to leave behind? What do they want to change? What scares them?

To create an example of a character manifesto, I'm going to take a tidbit from each of the three manifestos above and make them my character's stuff.

Example: My character now:

- Believes in asking the stupid question because the way a person answers will tell her what she really needs to know about their character. Are they kind?

- She believes she'll find the love of her life when she starts doing the things she loves. Only, she's not sure what she loves, so she asks everybody what their passion is and tries their passion on for size.

- Growing up the middle child, she's often felt ignored, so she embraces the idea that rebels can't be ignored.

- As such, she takes on the role of a rebel at work, because this is how you get the attention of the person who promotes you up the ladder.

After you've pulled from sample manifestos and created a list of your character's stuff, it's time to write a manifesto for the character.

Trick: don't reinvent the wheel. Find a manifesto whose rhythm appeals to you and mimic it. If it has five syllables in the first line, put five syllables in your first line. If there are seven syllables in the second line, put seven syllables in your second line. AND SO ON!

If there's a line in it that resonates with your character, use it, or something similar.

Example: up above, I listed a character's stuff based on the sample manifestos. Now, I'll turn the stuff into that character's manifesto.

Never fear the stupid question.

Fear the person who answers in a tone of ridicule.

Love finds you.

To search love out is to send it into hiding.

Steal passions from others until you find one you don't want to give back.

Then keep that sucker and do it with a passionate heart.

Do-gooders are ignored.

It's **the rebel who sits in the CEO seat.**

I am the CEO of my own life.

Now from her MANIFESTO, I'll pull out her obsessions (I've bolded them for you) and brainstorm a funny scene to go with the obsession. Don't groan (remember, I told you everyone can learn to write funny, but you have to put in the work. Well, this is some of the work. You must learn to locate sources of humor to include them in your books).

Example:

Based on the above character's manifesto, I'm going to say the following are her obsessions:

1. She's appalled at the idea of going on a blind date, because that's an act of searching for love. If someone were to set her up on a blind date without telling her, she'd immediately tell the guy "You're not now/nor ever will be the love of my life. Adiós." Which could be funny if she got it all wrong and it wasn't a blind date, but an impromptu job interview for her dream job.

2. Or let's say while she's in search of her passion, she decides to try out the trading-up trend on TikTok. She starts with trading a paperclip for a coffee cup. She trades the cup for a thermos. Her end goal is to trade for a house (this is an actual thing on TikTok).

One of her trades becomes the meet-cute for the book. Hmmm...how could it become the meet-cute?

3. Let's say her trade is with a teenager obsessed with this TikTok trend and the teenager trades my heroine a baseball signed by Babe Ruth. At this point, the father discovers what's happened and comes to undo the trade.

4. Because my character is obsessed with the idea that do-gooders (ones who would do the right thing and give the ball back) never go anywhere in life, she says no to the father who wants his ball back. This ball will, after all, go a long way in helping her eventually trade for a house.

5. At this point, the scene could go in many different directions, but since you're trying to add humor to your book, you're going to take it in the direction of funny. How would you do it?

Here's a manifesto I wrote for one of my actual book characters. The character's name is Aggie. Everything she does in the book *Aggie the Horrible Versus Max the Pompous Ass* is in line with her manifesto. This is the manifesto I wrote using the funny how-to guide I shared a link to above.

AGGIE THE HORRIBLE'S MANIFESTO

Stilettos are the devil's playground. Stilettos are a wink from God.

Crocs have no deity.

Secrets seldom stay under a rock.

Never settle.

People will come and go from your life. Trust none of them.

Except one.

Love. Doesn't. Survive. Between. Opposites.

Your parents will love you only if you're lovable.

Always sing in the shower. Never in the tub.

Always do the one thing that most scares you.

Search until you find, but hope for less than your soul desires.

Knowledge slays.

Felon.

As you can tell, this manifesto isn't full of fun stuff. But from it, I was able to pull out what Aggie obsesses over and turn it into several different funny scenes in my book. Aggie the Horrible obsesses over knowledge. She obsesses over fashion dos and don'ts. She obsesses over never settling. She obsesses over being realistic.

Not only did this manifesto dictate how Aggie went through life in this book, the actual manifesto ended up being included in a scene in my book, *Aggie the Horrible Versus Max the Pompous Ass*. Grab a copy of this book if you want to see how I pulled that one off.

ASSIGNMENT: Write a manifesto for a character in a book you're plotting. What obsessions can you pull from it that'll allow you to add humor hits to your novel?

ASSIGNMENT: Brainstorm scenes to go with these obsessions.

Seven

CIRCLING BACK

CIRCLING BACK

In the opening, I mentioned the nine things that cause a person to laugh. Six of them can be used to create laughter in our readers. They are:

1. Release

2. Negative Emotion

3. Recognition

4. Incongruity

5. Surprise

6. Superiority

The reason I'm reminding you of these is, you need to keep them in mind when you want your reader to laugh.

You'll need to craft your words into something that'll trigger one of the above laugh inducers.

And just so you know, most of the time you'll have a combination of two of those elements in play.

Comedians learn these, memorize them, and use them when creating jokes via the use of a laugh-inducing technique.

As you've learned earlier in this book, one of these techniques is the use of EXAGGERATION. This is simply the stretching of the truth or lie or situation.

While exaggeration is the most popular, there are oodles of other technique tools. Well, maybe not oodles, but oodles of names for the tool of their choice. In other words, what one comedian might call a potato, another might call a Vodka Martini. When you get to the gist of what's behind the name, the tool is the same. So whether you call it a stiletto or pump or loafer or sneaker, it's still a shoe.

Here's a chart of a few of the comedians I've studied and the tools they use.

Comedians and Their Favorite Tools to Create Comedy

DAVE FOX	LEIGH ANNE JASHEWAY	MARK SHATZ & MEL HELITZER	JERRY CORLEY	SCOTT DICKERS
Take of 3 →	List of three →	Triples		
U-turns →	Misdirection →	Reverses →	Reverses →	Misplaced focus
Superiority →		Superiority		
Twisted interpretation →	Definition →	Play on words →	Double Entendres →	Word play
Parallel →			Paired phrases	
	Twisted cliché →		Incongruity	
Fake statistics →	Exaggeration →	Exaggeration		Hyperbole →
	Observation →	Realism →	Observation/ recognition →	Reference
	Comparison →		Compare and → contrast	Analogy
			Slapstick →	Shock/madcap
			Irony →	Irony
Falsehoods	Motto		Simple Truth	
Uh-oh moments			Benign Retaliation	
Callback			Paradox	Parody
Self-deprecation				
False bravado				

Where you see the arrows, I'm pointing out that the comedians are indeed making use of the same technique, but they have different names for it.

In the next several chapters, I'll focus on a couple of the tools from each comedian's tool belts. And if you're shouting at the book, "I don't want to learn how to be a comedian, I want to learn how to add humor to my book!," stop shouting. Once I explain the funny tool, I'll give you examples of how you can make it work for you in your novels.

If you crave a more in-depth and complete look at the techniques of the above listed comedians, I strongly encourage you to buy their books or take their classes. I did. In fact, I studied humor for well over a year before I got busy trying to wrap my brain around how I could apply what I learned in my books.

At the end of this book, I'll give you a list of the resources I recommend.

Eight

COMEDIAN - DAVE FOX

COMEDIAN - DAVE FOX

I took an online class taught by Dave Fox entitled "The Art of Being Funny." In this class, he teaches twelve techniques for creating laughter. His class was one of the first I took when I went on my journey to learn how to write funnier. As such, he introduced me to a lot of the art of writing funny.

It was through his class I was first introduced to the idea of picking a mentor and shadow stalking them.

*Steve Martin also recommended having a mentor. As well as many others. Heck, Steve Martin isn't even mentioned in the chart from the previous chapter. I told you, I did a lot of research. I can't include it all, or this book wouldn't be short and to the point. Nevertheless, I do recommend Steve Martin's Masterclass on comedy writing.

One of the things that stuck with me from Dave Fox's class is, if you have to explain a punch line, it's not funny.

As a novelist who wants to add humor to your writing, it's important you keep this rule in mind. The reader's laughter should come at the end of the humor hit, not at the end of your explanation of the humor hit. DON'T EXPLAIN WHY IT WAS FUNNY.

One of the tools Dave Fox uses to make his audience laugh is fake statistics. He's a big believer in exaggerating or understating numbers.

Example:

Below, in a stripped-down dialogue stream, I've shown you an example of how you could add humor to your novel via **fake statistics**.

"Do you even like me?"

"Of course I like you."

"A lot?"

"Define 'a lot?'"

"Eighty percent of your emotions toward me have the emotion *like* in them."

"Define 'a little?'"

"Fifty percent."

"What would you call 'like' that weighs in at around a half-percent?"

"Pity like."

"I do pity the fool who likes you more than a half-percent."

You may read the above and shout, "That's not funny!" And you wouldn't be wrong. It needs some TLC-editing layers before it's truly funny, but it's an example of how you can get started in your quest to add funny to your writing via fake statistics.

Dave Fox also gives the tip to pause at the end of a punch line. The pause allows the audience time to laugh. As novelists, this would translate into starting a new paragraph.

Another of the laughter tools taught in Fox's class is the use of **False Bravado**. This is where you brag about yourself or your abilities in a way you don't really mean. The fact that you don't mean it has to be OBVIOUS.

The use of False Bravado makes a person laugh because what's being said/read is incongruent with what the listener/reader views as the reality of the situation. Remember, incongruity is one of the things that makes people laugh.

EXAMPLE: My husband, who's a retired social studies teacher, was LOVED by his students because of the humor he brought to the classroom. I met my husband when we both taught in the same high school and thus shared the same set of students. Our students saw us as two people who didn't mesh in the dating world. We were WAY incongruent in their young brains.

They saw him as the nerdy, weird, fun teacher and me as the high heel-wearing, strict business teacher. On many occasions, when a student would first learn of our relationship, they would come into his classroom and ask him, "Why would Ms. Wells ever date you?" My husband, using false bravado, would always respond - often while standing on his desk and striking a pose - "Because I am a sex god." Which cracked up his students because, well...while I love him like crazy, at no time in his life has he ever come across as a sex god to...his students. *Note: I realize today his saying that to students would probably get him in a mountain of trouble.

I tell you this story because it's a prime way novelists could use false bravado in their novels, simply by assigning the false bravado quirk to one of their characters.

It wouldn't have to be a major character. It could be a sidekick.

Nine

COMEDIAN – JERRY CORLEY

COMEDIAN –
JERRY COR-
LEY

Remember my mentioning I took an online Master-class by Steve Martin? In it, he refers his students to an article written by Jerry Corley entitled "13 Major Comedy Structures." This article is free, and it discusses a lot of the tools taught in the classes and books I read. Here, I've given you a couple of them, and how you can use them in your novel.

DOUBLE ENTENDRE – saying one thing that can be taken in two different ways.

Example: In your novel, you have a klutzy character who's about to go on a guided hike for the first time to gather information for an article she'll write for a travel magazine. When she arrives at the location where the hike is to begin, she discovers her guide is the **very same man** whose foot she'd dropped a hot cup of coffee on earlier in the morning. <u>Of course he is. I write romantic comedy.</u>

He has a walking stick with him. She's stressed the walking aid isn't something he normally uses on hikes, but instead an instrument to help him manage the pain of a scalded foot. In an attempt to discover if her fear is right, she says, "I bet you get a lot of compliments on your stick. Do you use it often?"

The man, who'll be the hero in my book, replies in a mock-shocked tone, "Are you asking me to stick and tell?" (his response uses double-entendre, play on words, and cliché twist)

Triples – If you've ever taken a Lawson Writer's Academy class taught by the fabulous Margie Lawson, you probably recognize this literary tool. Comedians use triples as a workhorse to hang a joke on. The tool is used simply by listing three things. The first two things go together, but the third thing doesn't (INCONGRUITY AT WORK), and (if it's funny) it surprises the reader, which results in a smirk or chuckle. While the third item is incongruent, it does have to fit in on some level. When readers discover how it fits in, that's when they laugh.

Example:

Setup: A couple is on a blind date. The guy is perfection to look at, and the woman immediately starts wondering why he needed to be set up on a blind date. What's wrong with him? There has to be something wrong with him (exaggeration at work).

At the very first opportunity, she blurts out, "Tell me what your last girlfriend would say are your flaws as a boyfriend?"

Without hesitating, the man replies, "I have a small dick, a smaller brain, and am a closet comedian" (three things were listed, and the last one is, on the surface, incongruent). *Note: I've resisted the urge to explain this joke. If you don't get it, you don't get it. Remember the rule that if you must explain it, it's not funny. Trust that your readers are smart enough to figure out your jokes. If, on occasion, some go over their head, that's okay. You'll get them with your next humor hit.

Moving on. Depending on how the man delivers his above response (sardonically, deadpan, with a twinkle in his eyes), the woman will have a multitude of internal thoughts (make these funny) that'll plague her during the rest of the meal.

In fact, her bombarding thoughts could lead to a dialogue tangent much like the one Darynda Jones set up in the first chapter of her book, *A Good Day for Chardonnay*.

Ten

COMEDIAN - LEIGH ANNE JASHEWAY

*COMEDIAN -
LEIGH ANNE
JASHEWAY*

S everal years ago, *Writer's Digest* offered a class taught by Jasheway. Sadly, when I went to find the link to the class, it appears the class is no longer taught. Which is too bad, because it was an excellent class. But I did come across an online article written for *Writer's Digest* by the marvelous Jasheway entitled "10 WAYS TO IMPROVE YOUR WRITING WHILE THINKING LIKE A COMEDIAN."

Item #10 on her list: **INCONGRUITY.** Jasheway says when incongruity is thrown at us, our brains get busy trying to figure out how they connect. And this is a good thing, because it holds your reader's attention. They're not bored if they're scrambling to find the connection. As novelists, we don't have to limit our use of this tool to triples. We can use it when we're describing a setting or brainstorming a plot point or developing a character quirk.

Example: This is an example from my life.

Once upon a time when I was a high school counselor, I had a young man and his parents in my office. The parents were enrolling their senior year son at our school. Why? Because he'd been at a Catholic school and they'd kicked him out. While hitting the print button on his new schedule, I decided to give him a pep talk. This is what I said.

"No one knows you here. This is a great chance for you to go in and give all your new teachers a good **blow job** and turn over a new leaf in your educational journey."

OF COURSE, I meant to say **snow job**. At this point, I got up and left my office to get paper for my printer (my printer didn't need paper, but I had to get out of there to compose myself).

This is what I imagine went on in my office while I stood in the hall hyperventilating. I imagine, at first, the family of three was confused by my **incongruent** statement for the young man to go forth and give his teacher's not just a blow job, but a good blow job. When their brains figured out I meant to say snow job, they were going to laugh—at least on the inside.

Later, once I'd survived the embarrassment of what I did, I was able to make others laugh as a result of an embarrassing moment in my life. Why did this story make others laugh? Because **NEGATIVE emotions** are one of the things that cause others to laugh. Yep, something that causes someone a negative emotion is fair game to use to make a reader laugh.

Note: The fact that this student was coming from a private Catholic school makes the whole thing even funnier. I say this to remind you to exaggerate, exaggerate, exaggerate when you invent your funny scenes.

ASSIGNMENT: Keep a notebook with the times you felt one of the lighter negative emotions. Those are: Embarrassment. Confusion. Frustration. Later, see if you can repurpose something from your life into your novel in a funny way.

I can easily take my blow job versus snow job debacle and place it in a romantic comedy in such a way that it'll make my readers laugh.

Have you had moments in your life you could repurpose into a scene in your book?

In the class I took with Jasheway, she suggested using a **Journalistic Association Chart** to come up with fun incongruity opportunities. This is a tool I've tried and had great success with. Here's how it works.

Create a table with six columns and four rows. Just like you learned in journalism class, on the top you're going to use the words: who; what; where; when; why/how. Down the left-hand side, you have:

1. Normal things you think of when thinking of the topic.

2. Unexpected things when thinking of your topic.

I've filled one out below to give you a feel for how it works. My topic is FASHIONISTA.

Topic - Fashionista					
	Who	What	Where	When	Why How
Normal things you think of when you think of a fashionista	Beautiful women Impossibly thin women Rich women	Clothes Hats Jewelry Selfie-sticks Stilettos	NYC Spas Magazines Nail-Salons	Fashion week Back to school First day of work	To feel beautiful To look important Rich To make an impression
Things you don't think of when thinking of a fashionista	Athletes Computer-Wiz Street-beggars Coupon-shoppers	Crocs Frumpy Flash-drives	Small-towns Gas-stations Rodeo Dollar-Store	In the rain At the laundromat Garage sale	No time for make up bank-rupt broke

When you're reading this chart, you'll see under the WHO column normal things you might think of when thinking about a fashionista are beautiful women, impossibly thin women, rich women. And then the unexpected things you might think about when thinking of fashionistas are athletes, street beggars, computer wiz kids, coupon shoppers.

Things in the lower half of the chart are incongruent with things in the upper half. How can you combine them in a way that brings humor to your reader?

This kind of chart could be what gave the creator of *Schitt's Creek* the idea to plop a rich, fashion-forward family down in the middle of an offensive-named small town (an offensive-named small town would be incongruent with a rich, fashion-forward family).

If you haven't watched that series, I recommend giving it a try. I didn't think I'd like it and resisted my daughter's urgings to watch it for over a year. I'm so glad she kept hounding me. The show is hilarious. I say that, but I'll also say it had some scenes that were truly slapstickish, and that isn't my humor taste. Nevertheless, the creators made up for those scenes with many other varieties of humor and a story line that made you eventually fall in love with those rich out-of-towners (fish-out-of-water trope with humor).

In the online class I took with Jasheway, she describes her preferred Eight Joke Types. Number three on her list is **MOTTO**.

MOTTO – A form of wordplay in which you're describing an organization, state, country, etc. To create a motto, you first need to:

1. Choose a group.
2. Make a list of their qualities (stereotypes).
3. Create your motto.

Her joke example was this: Harley Davidson – Here for you during your midlife crisis – Pinterest.

This is a super fun way for you to drop a humor hit into your novel.

Example: In my current novel, *The Undead Life of Molly Thorn*, her boss is the Grim Reaper for the Magicals. This is book one in the *Magical Midlife Moonlighting* series. I've listed below ten possible mottos for the Grim Reaper. Why ten? You know the answer. Repeat after me: Your first idea is seldom your best idea.

Which one would you pick? Or did you come up with a better one?

MOTTOS FOR THE GRIM REAPER TO THE MAGICAL

1. Here for you during your last bad decision.

2. Death – just do it.

3. Because you're dead.

4. Think Oooops.

5. Can you see me now?

6. Sometimes you feel like a breath...sometimes you don't.

7. What's in your past?

8. When it Absolutely, Positively has to end tonight.

9. Here to light up your life.

10. A death is a terrible thing to waste.

If you want to know if this kind of thing is worth the effort, the above exercise took me about five minutes, and it gave me an idea for a **repetition/call back joke** to end my *Magical Midlife Moonlighting* series.

In book one of my upcoming series, *Magical Midlife Moonlighting*, the heroine, who's the assistant to the Grim, can ask him a snarky question about his work motto and offer up one of the choices I listed above. In book two, the Grim might offer up his own as a defense for something he's done that's upset the heroine. Then in book three, somewhere on the last page, she announces her final decision on what his motto should be. I don't know if this is how it'll play out. At the moment, I'm simply real-time brainstorming to show you how the process works. What I do know is, I love the idea, and it WILL be a running humor hit in my series.

Eleven

COMEDIANS - MARK SHATZ AND MEL HELITZER

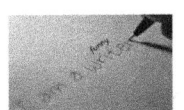

COMEDIANS - MARK SHATZ AND MEL HELITZER

U sing Themed Words to Add Humor to your writing

As an author who's taken one or two or a million classes on writing, I know to use **themed words** in my writing. My favorite of those above-mentioned classes was one taught via Lawson's Writer Academy by Elizabeth Essex, entitled: "It's All About Character, Using Character Themed Words."

Themed words are words that directly relate to your characters' unique life experiences. For instance, words associated with their careers, hobbies, or quirks. What I didn't necessarily think about when peppering in these themed words was how I could use them as humor hits in my writing.

That is, until I was reading *Comedy Writing Secrets*, by Mark Shatz with Mel Helitzer, and stumbled across a paragraph about how Humor Lecturer Art Glinner starts his seminars with **wordplay** as a way of getting his audience's creative juices flowing. What Glinner asks his audience to do is think of a career, then write words that might describe how they feel when they get home at night.

For example: A firefighter might feel out of oxygen. Or burned up. A chef might feel fried to a crisp.

When I taught my class on adding humor to your writing, this was one of my student's favorite assignments. They came up with such clever ways to describe their tired characters.

ASSIGNMENT: Create a broad themed word list for your characters based on their stuff...like their careers or hobbies. Now, use those words to make a top ten list in the following categories:

1. How they feel when they come home from work.

   a.

   b.

c.

d.

e.

f.

g.

h.

i.

2. How they feel after sex.

a.

b.

c.

d.

e.

f.

g.

h.

3. How they feel after a break-up.

a.

b.

c.

d.

e.

f.

g.

h.

4. How they feel after meeting their love interest.

a.

b.

c.

d.

e.

f.

g.

h.

If you're not writing romance, adjust the list to fit what you are writing. Perhaps how they feel after capturing the bad guy. Or how they feel after cutting loose the baggage that's been holding them back in life. Or how they feel when they finally manage to say something clever to their arch nemesis.

I have a future book planned that has a lawyer as the heroine. I went through the above wordplay process to come up with a list of funny swear words a lawyer might use. Here are the top three I settled on for this future heroine:

1. Blasted Misdemeanor.
2. Holy Frackin' Indictment.
3. Flamin' Affidavit.

Now that you have this tool in your toolbox and you've created a list of ten items in each column, go forth and add humor to your novel by finding a place to drop in how your character feels with this exercise in mind.

Example: Soon to be released: *The Impromptu Nanny Contract* has a former fashion influencer character who's now a temporary nanny. The scene opens with her boss, the child's parent, returning from work. He looks as fresh as a freaking lemon drop martini. She, on the other hand, looks like something a drunken tornado regurgitated.

I want to make use of themed words in this scene as a way of adding a touch of humor to the situation. Here's my chart on words associated with a nanny:

Nanny themed words	Play Parks Children	Lunch Time Pickup-line Naps	Therapist Uniforms	Deprived of adult convo.
Teaching Art Projects Tears	Schedules Planners Juggling time	tissues bullies	Helping with homework	Mean girls

And here's the scene:

Mr. Darby stood in the doorway, looking as fresh as a freaking lemon drop martini, and surveyed her. His left eyebrow inched toward his hairline.

"Dare I ask how your day went?"

Of course he dared. He no doubt loved seeing her at her worst. It was, after all, why he'd forced her into the position of nanny for his precocious six-year-old in the first place.

She bit back the two-word response that begged to leap off her tongue. "Hmmm...let me think about it. We made noodle art Christmas gifts. Unfortunately, the two-pound bag of elbow noodles flew everywhere when your daughter insisted on opening it herself."

His lips twitched.

"Then while in the middle of gluing those slippery little son-of-a-suckers on construction paper, the lid magically fell off the glue bottle, and a glob of the sticky stuff landed on your daughter's project."

"Why didn't you—"

"At which point, she screamed and pushed madly at the glue marring her masterpiece."

"My little perfectionist."

He said that like it was a good thing. It wasn't. Perfectionism led to uptightism.

Is that a word? If not, it should be.

"When I turned my head to procure a wet wipe, she reached out her chubby, glue-covered hand, caught my ponytail, and pulled."

His brow furrowed. "That's unfortunate. I thought she'd gotten past the urge to pull others' hair. Please let her therapist know when you take her to her appointment tomorrow."

The mean-girl-in-the-making didn't need a therapist. She needed a parent who had time for her. "I'll be sure and do that."

"May I fix you a drink?" He strolled past her to the bar cart. "You look...played out."

Played out. Wasn't he just a well-dressed clown?

"No, thank you. I have a much-needed adult playdate lined up. I'm sure Charles will have a delightful plan to revive my waning friskiness."

It was a lie. Charles didn't exist, but Mr. Darby didn't need to know that. Her lack of candidates for adult activities wasn't any of her boss's business.

Twelve

SPECTACLE SCENE

SPECTACLE
SCENE

S omewhere in my pursuit to learn all there is to know about writing a great book, I learned about the **spectacle scene**. I wish I could tell you who first introduced me to this concept, but I simply can't recall. A spectacle scene is a scene everyone talks about when your book has ended, or the movie is over, or the Netflix series is over.

In *A Few Good Men*, it's the court scene when Jack Nicholson admits he ordered the Code Red.

In the movie *When Harry Met Sally*, the spectacle scene is the café-orgasm scene.

In the movie *Steel Magnolias*, the spectacle scene is right after the funeral, when Clairee Belcher offers up Ouiser Boudreau as a punching bag for the grieving mother to punch. **By the way, if you recall, one of the reasons people laugh is for release.** In *Steel Magnolias*, this funeral scene (the spectacle scene) offers a release for the audience, who's been sobbing up until this moment in the funeral scene. The fact that there was so much grief leading up to this moment makes the scene even funnier than it might have been if done at a different point in the movie.

If the genre you write in isn't normally funny, a release scene might be a place for you to add a slap of humor in your novel. I say slap, not hint, because if amusement is the emotion you want to pull out of your readers in your spectacle scene, you can't half-a** it. You've got to go all in. Your intent is for the readers to mention this scene when they tell others why they must, must, must read your book.

Of course, these examples are pulled from movies. What are some spectacle scenes you recall from books? Those scenes that stayed with you long after you closed the book? Go back and analyze that scene. If it made you laugh, what type of scene did it follow?

You should strive to have one spectacle scene in each of your books. Again, the spectacle scene is an excellent place to put to use all the tools you've learned on how to add humor to your writing. This is a place to go all in and really pull the laughter out of your readers.

Thirteen

WORD CHOICES

*WORD
CHOICES*

Research shows our brains are wired to find **words with a K or hard C** sound in them as funny. This was first mentioned by Neil Simon when speaking about his play *The Sunshine Boys*. I learned about it while reading the book *Comedy Writing Secrets*.

The research behind the why of this isn't important. What is important is, using words with the phonetic sounds of K & hard C will up your reader's perception of how funny you are as a writer.

Note: Unlike punch lines, which ALWAYS come at the end of a joke, place your K&C words in the middle of your sentences.

The names you give your characters are an easy way to add humor to your novel.

In the movie *Steel Magnolias*, the town's Southern-themed character is named Clairee Belcher. The town's curmudgeon is Ouiser Boudreaux. Their names clue the reader in to the fact that they're going to be fun characters to read about.

The title of your book is another prime spot for a humor hit.

My book, *Aggie the Horrible Versus Max the Pompous Ass*, practically screams this is a fun romp of a read.

When **describing a town or character** or anything, try to use funny words. For example: Uggabugga is a much funnier name for a store than Five and Dime. Or order a frankfurter instead of a hot dog at the Dairy Queen.

Use a **double entendre when naming stores**: If you recall from earlier in the book, a double entendre is when a word or phrase could have two interpretations. Add humor to your novel by naming your stores things like "Thai Tanic" or "Tequila Mockingbird." If you want a good laugh, here's a <u>link</u> to titles of books with unintentional double entendres: https://forreadingaddicts.co.u k/language/20-unintentional-innuendo-book-titles/

Fourteen

COMEDIAN - SCOTT DIKKERS

*COMEDIAN -
SCOTT
DIKKERS*

C omedian Scott Dikkers says, "You never state the subtext. It's called subtext because it's concealed under the text and never revealed except inside the reader's mind." As a novelist, you already know this. But when it comes to creating a joke (a humor hit in your novel), there are some nuances worth mentioning.

According to Dikkers, there are 11 funny filters comedians can use to **veil** their subtext. The veil allows the reader to figure out the subtext. You can read all about these eleven filters in his book, *How to Write Funny*. It's a book that leans heavily on the side of teaching comedians how to write jokes. But I was able to pull from it a way to add humor to my novels.

Irony is one of his eleven funny filters. When using irony to add humor to your novel, you have a non-point-of-view character say something in a <u>tone full of conviction and with a straight face</u>. There's no hint given to the listener/reader of the character's true thoughts on the subject.

Readers will laugh when they put two and two together and understand what the speaker didn't say. Why does it have to happen in the non-POV's head? Because if you're in the POV of the character speaking, his internal thoughts will reveal the subtext. At this point, you'd have used sarcasm to generate a laugh, not irony. According to Dikkers, "Sarcasm is irony light."

You may be wondering, how do you have a character say something with one hundred percent conviction and the reader know he doesn't mean it? You have him exaggerate.

Confused? Let's give this a whirl.

Example: First, your character must have a strong opinion on something. You can pull these strong opinions from the manifesto you wrote on your character.

Let's say my character believes the career of nannies exists because there are so many parents who would give their child the whole world - minus, of course, the hours and days and years the parent needs to live their life unencumbered by said child.

And we're in the POV of a parent who's just discovered this is what the other character does for a living. The

POV parental character asks the nanny what she thinks of parents who leave their children with nannies.

Nanny responds using irony, "Nannies are absolutely vital in the world we live in. After all, we entrust our money to bankers. Why not our children to nannies?"

Nanny responds using **sarcasm,** "A nanny's role is to nurture and love your most precious possession during those absolutely inescapable moments when you're not to be disturbed." We're still in the other character's POV, but the nanny's response is **sarcasm because her opinion is thinly veiled.** The "when you're not to be disturbed" is too on-the-nose to reach the status of irony.

Fifteen

FUNNY PREMISES

*FUNNY
PREMISES*

Premise – If you want to add humor to your novels, a sure-fire way to make that an easy-peasy activity versus a calculus-while-drunk-and-standing-on-your-head activity is to have a funny premise for your novel.

The premise is your elevator pitch for the book.

One of the best places to find examples of premise is on <u>imbd.com</u>. You'll discover the movie's logline (premise) next to the movie poster, just under the title and star rating. I suggest you look at the loglines for movies and see what kind of funny story idea your brain comes up with as a result of that logline.

Example: Using the loglines of several movies, I'll real-time rethink them into a humorous book idea.

Movie: *Don't Look Up*. Logline: Two low-level astronomers must go on a giant media tour to warn mankind of an approaching comet that'll destroy Planet Earth.

I imagine this as: Two low-level Cayman Island weathermen must go on the Weather Channel and convince the world the perfect winter storm is about to hit the world on the same day.

Show: *The Golden Girls*. Logline: Four previously married women live together in Miami, sharing their various experiences together and enjoying themselves despite hard times.

I imagine this as: Four has-been movie heartthrobs, striving to appear relevant in Hollywood, live together in a run-down mansion, where they're secretly making a living writing a series of books dictated to them by the mansion's moody resident ghost.

Movie: *Only Murders in the Building*. Logline: Three strangers who share an obsession with true crime suddenly find themselves caught up in one.

I imagine this as: Three teenagers who hate their history class suddenly find themselves in possession of a time-traveling app.

Show: *Schitt's Creek*. Logline: When rich video store magnate Johnny Rose and his family suddenly find themselves broke, they're forced to leave their pampered lives to regroup in Schitt's Creek.

I imagine this as: When three street urchins are plucked off the streets to be the public faces of the actual children to a paranoid billionaire couple, they're forced to live a public lie while striving to make sense of the lifestyle of the rich and ridiculous.

All the premises I've reimagined have lots of room for me to add characters with comedic traits and obsessions and fun settings and scenes into a novel. By starting with a comedic premise, I've set myself up to write a book full of humor hits. This won't work if you're writing in a traditionally non-funny genre, but for those of you who do, this tool is for you.

Now it's your turn.

ASSIGNMENT: Look at the premises of movies in the same genre you write. Then reimagine those premises as one of your future books. A worksheet is provided.

Name of Movie	Their Premise	Your Premise
Name of Movie	Their Premise	Your Premise
Name of Movie	Their Premise	Your Premise
Name of Movie	Their Premise	Your Premise
Name of Movie	Their Premise	Your Premise

Sixteen

IMMEDIATE REVERSES

*IMMEDIATE
REVERSES*

W hile researching reverses as a comedy technique taught by Jerry Corley, I stumbled across a
blog post written by Stephen Hoover entitled "Comedy
Techniques: The Immediate Reverse." I thought it would
give me examples of jokes using the reverses technique
mentioned by Jerry Corley in *13 Comedy Structures*; it
didn't. What it did was show how a sitcom writer used
a technique called immediate reverse to create humor
in character dialogue. The writer is Stan Daniels. And
the technique is where a character says something, then
does an immediate 180-degree shift in his stance.

How to set up an Immediate Reverse:

1. Heartfelt statement from Character A.

2. Influencing action occurs.

3. Character A says something that's the complete opposite of the opening statement.

Example: 1972 Burt Reynolds private eye movie *Shamus*.

BURT (indignantly): "You think you can buy me??"

GANGSTER: "I'll pay you twenty-five thousand dollars cash."

BURT: "Congratulations. You just bought me."

As an author, I can tell you, I will use this technique in my upcoming book, *The Impromptu Nanny Contract*.

I challenge you to try and utilize this in your manuscript the next time you want to add a humor hit to your novel.

And since I brought it up, there's a comedic technique called **reverses**. Not to be confused with immediate reversals. Reverses in comedy is when the joke is going in one direction, causing the listener to expect a certain outcome, but then flips. The flip doesn't have anything to do with a character's stance on a situation. The flip is just that the ending to the joke or story that the character is telling is the opposite of what was expected.

Examples:

"I practice safe sex—I use an airbag." Garry Shandling

"Last week, my house was on fire. My wife told the kids, 'Be quiet, you'll wake up Daddy.'" Rodney Dangerfield.

In those jokes, the second half doesn't match what one would expect.

As authors, we can use this technique in our dialogue. It'll require brainstorming.

1. Start by coming up with a topic/situation two characters might talk about. Something relatable.

2. Then, think of what you want your twist ending to be.

3. From there, work backward and set up the story a character is telling.

Live-brainstorming:

1. Let's say the topic is men who are intimidated by powerful women.

2. You want the punch line to be the female character simply couldn't care less.

3. Working backward from the punch line, I came up with the following dialogue:

"A clever, powerful woman knows how to handle a man who feels insecure about their societal status gap: She dumps him."

Seventeen

SYLLOGISMS

SYLLOGISMS

When I took the Masterclass on comedy given by Steve Martin, he referred his students to an article called "The Syllogisms of Seinfeld," written by Joe Carter.

I'm going to be honest with you, the article made my brain hurt. And because I'm not big on brain hurt, the first time I read it, I didn't get much out of the article. I simply didn't want to put in the brain power to concentrate as much as the article required.

While compiling my information for this book, I stumbled back across the article and decided to conquer the beast. Brain hurt be damned.

Basically, the article says every time logic or fallacy is used in humor, it's playing one of three roles: Essence; Enhancer; Mechanism.

•

Essence: Either the use of logic or fallacy is what makes the joke funny.

- Enhancer: Either the use of logic or fallacy ADDS to the crux of what's funny and makes it funnier.

- Mechanism – Either the use of logic or fallacy is what propels the dialogue from one comment to another.

Hang with me, readers, I promise, I'm getting to the point where you'll discover how to take this dry information and add humor to your dialogue.

Under the umbrella of essence (that's where you use logic or fallacy to make something funny), you've got three types of jokes.

1. <u>Equivocation</u> – This is where one person says something and it can be interpreted in more than one way.

Example from Seinfeld:

Jerry and Father Curtis in "The Yada Yada."

"I wanted to talk to you about Dr. Whatley. I have a suspicion that he's converted to Judaism purely for the jokes."

"And this offends you as a Jewish person?" (1st logical interpretation)

"No, it offends me as a comedian." (2nd logical interpretation)

Now that you have an example, you can study it and practice writing a dialogue bit that copies the formula for essence/equivocation.

Remember from previous sections of this book, your first attempt may suck. It usually takes ten tries to find something that works.

Here's my 1st attempt for *The Impromptu Nanny Contract*.

"Can you believe he asked me to go on vacation with him and be the nanny for his spoiled five-year-old over Christmas?"

"And you're offended because you think his true intentions are to seduce you?"

"No. I think his true intentions are not to seduce me."

2. <u>Contradiction</u> – A dialogue that leans on the absurd side via the use of contradiction.

Example: Seinfeld - George discussing a massage given by a male masseuse with Elaine in "The Note."

"What if something happens?"

"What could happen?"

"What if it felt good?"

"It's supposed to feel good."

"I don't want it to feel good."

"Then why get the massage?"

"Exactly!"

Using my book, *The Impromptu Nanny Contract* - which I haven't even plotted as of the writing of this book - here's a first-attempt imagined scene between my heroine and her best friend using the above dialogue formula.

"I think you should say yes to being his nanny."

"What if something happened?"

"What could happen?"

"What if I'm good at being a nanny?"

"You're supposed to be good. That's what you do for a living."

"I don't want to be good at it."

"Then why did you become a nanny?"

"Exactly."

3. <u>False Cause</u> – This is when one assumes because A has preceded B, A caused B.

Example: Kramer and Jerry in "The Andrea Doria."

"No doctors for me. A bunch of lackeys and yes-men all towing the company line. Plus, they botched my vasectomy."

"They botched it?"

"I'm even more potent now!"

1st attempt - *The Impromptu Nanny Contract*

"I'll take a construction worker over a businessman any day. Those guys are a bunch of dick-led egotistical men. Plus, the one I dated in college ruined my metabolism."

"Ruined it?"

"Before him, I'd never topped the scale above one-twenty."

<u>Under the umbrella of Enhancer</u> – This is when the use of logic or fallacy ups how funny what is being said is, giving you hasty generalizations.

Example: Elaine and Jerry in "The Wink."

"So, what you're saying is that ninety to ninety-five percent of the population is undateable?"

"Undateable!"

"Then how are all these people getting together?"

"Alcohol."

***The Impromptu Nanny Contract* – 1st Attempt**

"So, you're saying your boss is one hundred percent the spawn of the devil and his daughter is one hundred percent the spawn of God?"

"One hundred percent!"

"How is that genetically possible?"

"He kidnapped her."

Under the Role of Mechanism – The logic or fallacy gets you from one thought to the next.

Jerry and Elaine in "The Red Dot."

"What are you saying?"

"I'm not saying anything."

"You're saying something."

"What could I be saying?""Well, you're not saying nothing. You must be saying something."

"If I was saying something, I would've said it."

"Why don't you say it?"

"I said it."

"What did you say?"

"Nothing."

1st attempt - *The Impromptu Nanny Contract*

"What did that look mean?"

"It didn't mean anything."

"It said something."

"What could it be saying?"

"Well, it didn't say nothing. It must have said something."

"If I gave you a look that said something, I'd make sure you heard it."

"Why don't you just tell me what it said?"

"I just did."

"What did it say?"

"I didn't give you a look."

*Note: If we met at a conference and you asked me to explain syllogisms, I still couldn't do it. But if you make note of the examples (theirs, not mine), then all you have to do is plug in your words to fit the formula. That's what I did.

Eighteen

ONE LINERS

ONE LINERS

When it comes to adding humor to your writing, one-liners are your besties. A one-liner is a factual statement with a joke attached. In *Comedy Writing Secrets*, by Mark Shatz with Mel Helitzer, it's noted that "Humor isn't about fun."

What I take from this as a novel writer is, what I put on the page won't be funny out of context. It will be funny in context. In other words, I'm not writing jokes. I'm writing dialogue and thoughts that'll tickle my readers, not my characters. This will often be done with witty one-liners (sometimes they have two or three lines, and that's okay).

ASSIGNMENT: Research one-liners that make you laugh.

ASSIGNMENT: Research one-liners that make your target audience laugh. You can pull these from the pages of bestsellers or movies in your genre.

Remember, what makes you laugh may not make your reader laugh. You're writing your book for the reader.

ASSIGNMENT: Use your discovered one-liners—all of them—to come up with new ones of your own. Do this by making note of any formula that's being used, then copy the formula - not the joke. Just like I did with syllogisms. NEVER THE JOKE. Don't skimp on this assignment. Find a hundred quotes and reimagine them all with the thought to make them funny.

EXAMPLE:

Here's a one (THREE)-liner out of the movie *The Big Lebowski*. "This is not 'Nam. This is bowling. There are rules."

And how I reimagined it for a potential line in *Aggie the Horrible Versus Max the Pompous Ass*: "This is not a high-dollar country club. This is a hole-in-the-wall bar. They're picky about who they welcome" (a version of this did make it into the book).

Here's another example of a one-liner - this one from *Goldmember 2002*, and how I reimagined it: "There are only two things I hate in this world: people who are intolerant of other people's culture and the Dutch."

And this is how I reimagined it for *Aggie the Horrible Versus Max the Pompous Ass*: "There are two things I hate: People who are intolerant of other people's choice of footwear and Crocs" (a version of this does show up in *Aggie the Horrible* as well).

Here are a couple of links to well-known one-liners:

This one is from BookBub, entitled "The 100 Most Iconic Book Quotes": https://www.bookbub.com/blog/famous-book-quotes

This one is from Parade, entitled "50 Funny Movie Quotes": https://parade.com/1120092/stephanieosmanski/funny-movie-quotes/

Nineteen

FACTUAL STATEMENTS

FACTUAL STATE-MENTS

I said in the last chapter one-liners are factual statements with jokes attached to the end. How do you, as an author, come up with those factual statements? Easy. Brainstorming. You begin by making a list of factual statements relating to your character's hobbies, career, the theme of your story, etc.

Once you have a list, work at attaching a punch line to each statement. If you do this prior to starting your writing, you may come up with scene ideas.

For instance: Factual statements about firefighters:

Their house has a pole.

Fire excites them.

They run into danger.

They smell like smoke.

If you were writing a story with a hero who's a fire-fighter in it, I'd be playing around with these statements and have them ready with a funny attachment for your heroine to use.

Example:

The heroine might say to the hero, "My mom always told me to marry a fireman. He'd be sure to have a pole worth sliding down."

Here is me doing this assignment in real-time. Pretend I'm plotting a book with a reporter in it.

Factual statements about reporters:

Everything is fair game.

Nothing is off limits.

When you talk, they listen.

Reports on things people don't have a clue about.

Always have pen and paper.

Deadlines.

Quoting sources.

Hot story ideas.

Word count.

Retractions.

Viable sources.

Headline.

Byline.

Reports on celebrity deaths.

Based on the above, here are my first three attempts to come up with something funny:

1. Mother says to her daughter, "Date a reporter – when you talk, he'll listen."

2. Conversation right after sex:

Her: "Sweet baby Jesus, you have divine power in the orgasm realm."

Him/reporter: "May I quote you on that?"

3. Reporter on a talk show interrupts a segment to say, "This just in: According to my sources, Lord Master Baiter has died. His closest friend, Madonna, said she will be in mourning for the foreseeable future and to please allow her time to grieve in private." He pauses, then glances at his co-host, who's laughing so hard, tears are streaming down his face, and scowls. "Why are you laughing? This is sad news."

Co-host, whose face is blotchy with red spots, gasps out, "Do you even know who this lord was?"

"Of course I do. He's from England and was someone very close to Madonna, and that's why he's on our radar."

"Dude, since when do we report on dead vibrators?"

The above examples are first attempts and need drastic editing. But I want you to see how one goes about working out their funny bone. Yes, being funny can be taught, but just like with driving, you've got to do your homework to get good at out-running the cops.

Twenty

NEVER SETTLE

*NEVER SET-
TLE*

I n case you've done a lot of skimming up until this
paragraph, let me say one more time: Never settle
on the first punch line that comes to mind. Sure, it
may be funny. But could it be funnier? Test your word
choices. Listen to it out loud. Is the cadence right? Is
your verbiage flabby? Remember, funny occurs in the
edits.

After you've written your novel, *highlight your humor
hits, and check each one of them for potential improve-
ment.*

One of the things I look for when checking my humor
hits is, did I kill the pacing of the scene just to be funny?
Why do I have to check for this? Because my editor
(whom I adore) tells me I'm guilty of the crime. UGH.

When a humor hit kills your pacing and you can't slim it down, kill the humor hit.

YOU NEVER SACRIFICE PACING FOR FUNNY.

Twenty-One

STRENGTHEN YOUR FUNNY BONE

STRENGTH-EN YOUR FUNNY BONE

Throughout this book, I've given you a lot of tools you can now use to add humor to your novel. But I'm not done. There are more. In this section, we're going to take another look at the one-liner. Why? Because it's that important.

Plus, in this chapter you'll learn about the use of:

- **Understatement.**

- **Recognition.**

- **Simple truths.**

- **Reverses.**

- **Twisted clichés.**

The one-liner – revisited. This tool will be your go-to when it comes to adding humor to your novel. Below, in the first half of the table, I've listed some famous one-liners.

ASSIGNMENT: Beneath each example, create your own funny line by using the one above it as a guide.

In a perfect world, this exercise will allow you to write a line you can then slip into your current work in progress. In an imperfect world, you'll save it for later use. Either way, be sure and save your creations.

NOTE: MARK them as your creations. I say this because I have notes of one-liners I'm pretty sure are my creative work, but I'm not 100%, so I can't use them on the off-chance I didn't create them (if you read this and laughed because you're also guilty of something similar, then this would be an example of recognition humor, which we'll discuss in this chapter).

After you've done the above assignment, in the remaining blank lines create your own one-liners that follow the example's formula.

I've filled in six to get you started. But you should do those six in your notebook with your own one-liners.

Reimagined One-Liners

Theirs   "It's the possibility of having a dream come true that
makes life interesting. ~The Alchemist by Paulo Coelho

Mine   "It's the thought of making your brows furrow
that prompts me to try." – Lisa Wells (future enemies-to-lovers book)

Theirs   "One morning I shot an elephant in my pajamas.
How he got in my pajamas I don't know." Animal Crackers (1930)

Mine   "One morning I woke up and kissed the man of my dreams.
Let me be the cautionary tale to dream bigger."
Lisa Wells ~future book

Theirs   "There's no crying in baseball!"
A League of Their Own (1992)

Mine   "There's no do-overs in parenting."
The Impromptu Nanny Contract – Lisa Wells

Reimagined One-Liners

Theirs   "Greed for lack of a better word is good."
          Wall Street (1987)

Mine   "Love for all its hype sucks." ~Lisa Wells (future book)

Theirs   "You know how to whistle don't you Steve? You just put
          your lips together and blow." To Have and Have Not (1945)

Mine   "You know how to say no, don't you Molly? You just raise your right
          hand and drop all but your middle finger."
          ~Lisa Wells (future book in the Magical Midlife Moonlighting series)

Theirs   "You're gonna need a bigger boat." Jaws
          (1975)

Mine   "You're gonna need a bigger dick." Lisa Wells (Future
          book)

Reimagined One-Liners

Theirs   **"I wish I knew how to quit you."**
Brokeback Mountain (2005)

Yours

Theirs   **"You make me want to be a better man."**
As Good As It Gets (1997)

Yours

Theirs   **"Well, nobody's perfect."**
Some Like It Hot (1959)

Yours

Understatement. You've learned the importance of exaggeration and how that technique helps you elicit laughter in your readers. The opposite of that is the understatement. It's a technique you can easily pop into your dialogue anytime you want to add a hint of humor to your novel. A character will say something nowhere near accurate—in an understated way.

Here are a couple examples of understatement:

1. *Apollo 13* - 1995

"Houston, we have a problem."

2. *The Good Place*:

Michael: "Just wanna double-check, how do ethical philosophers feel about murder?"**Chidi:** "It's frowned upon."

ASSIGNMENT: Go back to your one-liner assignment. Can you change several of them into understatement humor?

Open your current work in progress and insert one instance of an understatement.

Recognition Humor. In the opening of this book, it was pointed out recognition is one of the reasons people laugh. Recognition laughter occurs when something is said the reader/listener identifies with as something they've also done or thought.

Here are some examples of Recognition Humor:

1. "I'm just a stomach flu away from my goal weight." (*The Devil Wears Prada*, 2006)

2. "Just what is the handicapped parking situation at the Special Olympics? Is it still just the two spaces?" (*Seinfeld*)

Simple Truth Humor – There are times when we think things but don't say them. And most of the time, this is best. Once in a while, if the situation is safe for total truth, you might say what's on your mind. For this to be funny, what you say can't be done with a mean spirit.

Here's an example of Simple Truth Humor:

1. "It's the first time I've ever seen you look ugly. And that makes me kind of happy." (*Bridesmaids*, 2011)

ASSIGNMENT: Create a simple truth humor hit for your current WIP. Do it now, while you have a sample in front of you.

Example: Here's one I did for my WIP, *The Impromptu Nanny Contract*.

"Why are you laughing? This isn't funny."

"It's the first time you've ever been the one dumped. And that makes me kind of in the mood for champagne."

Twisted Cliché. This is something Margie Lawson teaches as a way of writing a damn good book. In comedy, the twist to the cliché bends on the funny side. When you do this, your reader will laugh or smirk, or at least give you a nod for doing what you did.

Example: "Where there's a will, there's a family fighting over it." Buzz Nutley

ASSIGNMENT: Below, I've listed clichés. Go ahead and twist them and include them in a book. I showed you how it's done with the first several.

1. Someone woke up on the wrong side of the bed. (Cliché)

"Someone woke up on the wrong side of the track." (Lisa Wells's future "across the track" romance)

2. Fit as a fiddle. (Cliché)

"Fit as a fiddle that's been left out in the rain." (Lisa Wells's future dialogue for an older character in her *Midlife Moonlighting* series)

3. All bark and no bite. (Cliché)

"Are you all bark and no delight when it comes to seduction?" (Lisa Wells's future dialogue in *The Magical Midlife of Molly Thorn*)

4. Her Knight In Shining Armor. (Cliché)

***Her Night In Shining Armani* (Lisa Wells's future book title of a new romantic comedy)**

5. I love you more than life itself. (Cliché)

Your   twisted   interpretation:

_____

6. He has nerves of steel. (Cliché)
Your   twisted   interpretation:

_____

7. Been there. Done that. (Cliché)
Your   twisted   interpretation:

_____

Twenty-Two

FUNNY SOUNDING WORDS

FUNNY
SOUNDING
WORDS

Adorbs	Biblioklept	Cankles	Conniption	Everywhen
Bamboozled	Blubber	Cattywampus	Cutesy-poo	Fartlek
Bazinga	Buccaneer	Collywobbles	Dingy	Festooned
Bevy	Bumfuzzle	Conjubilant	Dollop	Fiddle dee-dee
Finagle	Foppish	Gardyloo	Gumption	Hoi
Flabbergast	Frippery	Gobbledygook	Gunky	Hornswoggled
Fibbertigibbet	Fuddy-duddy	Gobsmacked	Hitherto	Hullabaloo
Flummoxed	Futz	Grog	Hodgepodge	Indubitably

An easy way to add humor hits to your writing is by using funny words in your characters' thoughts and dialogue. When you're creating your characters, have one of them bend toward the funny-word choice side.

Janky Kabob Kerplunk Knickers	Lackadaisical Lickety-split Lil-willie Lollygag	Loopy Mollycoddle Namby pamby Noggin	Noob Pantaloons Passel Persnickety	Piffle Polloi Popinjay Puggle
Ragamuffin Ramshackle Rapscallion Rookery	Rumpus Scalawag Schmooze Scotch	Scuttlebutt Smaze Snarky Sozzled	Squeegee Titter Tookus Waddle Walkabout Weasel	Whatnot Whippersnapper Widdershins Wishywashy Wonky Zazzy

Twenty-Three

CHEAT SHEET

*CHEAT
SHEET*

Here's a list of everything I've taught you. I'd like to say it's a list of everything you've learned, but I know a slew of you didn't do the homework.

If you're a part of that mickle, now is a good time to go back and do the homework.

At the very least, have this book on your desk when you're writing. Then, when you need to add humor, grab it, find a technique you want to use, and create something sure to make your readers laugh.

THE ROOT CAUSE OF LAUGHTER IN YOUR READERS:

- Release

- Negative

-

Emotions

- Recognition

- Incongruity

- Surprise

PLACES TO FIND FUNNY IDEAS:

- Instagram accounts

- TikTok accounts

- Facebook

- Twitter Accounts

- Journalist Association Chart

- Brainstorming

- Notebook of ideas

- T-shirts

- Memes

- People watching

- Reimagining funny premises

TOOLS TO CREATE YOUR HUMOR HITS:

- Call back/repetition subtext

- Character traits and motivations ramped up to the level of obsession

- Cliché twists

- Comedic premise

- Exaggeration

- Factual statements

- Fake statistics

- Funny sounding words

- Irony

- List of three

- Manifesto

- Motto

- Names of: Towns, establishments, characters

- Negative emotion

- One-liners

- Reversals

- Reverses

- Spectacle scene

- The fab five comedic characters

- Twisted interpretation

- Understatement

- Wordplay/Double Entendres

- Words that start with a K or hard C

In my blurb, I promised you twelve tools to help you add humor to your novel. Surprise, I gave you twenty-three. This way, if one of them just doesn't make sense to you, it's okay. I didn't short-humor you on my promise.

Now that you have the tools, go forth and create laughter in the world.

Twenty-Four

ASSIGNMENT CHEAT SHEET

ASSIGN-MENT CHEAT SHEET

I f you're like me, and you don't do the homework when you're first reading a book on the craft of writing, here are all the assignments in one location.

ASSIGNMENT: What Makes Your Readers Laugh?

Record your answers to the above question in a notebook or computer file.

ASSIGNMENT: Pick the first chapter of one of your Humor Guide's books, and study it in-depth. Keep a running tally of how many humor hits they have in chapter one. If they average 30 humor hits in the first chapter, then that's your goal with your books. If they have only one or two, then that's your goal. THE NUMBER OF HUMOR HITS WILL VARY BY GENRE. If they have no humor hits in their first chapter, then read the whole book and see how many they have in the book. Some genres may have only a half-dozen.

ASSIGNMENT: If you want extra credit, take the above assignment a step further and rate the humor hits. Are they lip-twitchers? Giggle inducers? Or snort-il-licit-drugs-out-of-your-nose causers? This extra credit step will let you know what level of humor you need to aim to achieve.

ASSIGNMENT: From now until your visit to the Pearly Gates (or the Gates you imagine seeing in your afterlife), every time you read something that causes you to snort chocolate milk or chardonnay or brain matter out of your nose, PLEASE write it down, analyze it, and understand how the reader pulled it off.

BONUS ASSIGNMENT: Start a new page in your journal, and write down what you see on T-shirts, funny signs, memes, etc., that would make your reader laugh. Repurpose the material for use as dialogue and charac-ter thoughts in your novels.

ASSIGNMENT: After you've read the first chapter of a book written by your chosen Humor Guide, take the time to reflect upon their techniques. Then brainstorm on how you can incorporate one of their techniques into one of your books. DON'T steal. Make it your own.

ASSIGNMENT: Create a laughter file and add at least three things a week to this file. Don't be lazy. Do this assignment. You'll thank me later.

ASSIGNMENT: Now that you have some traits (pictured below) with which to work, pick five of them that could pertain to a character in a book you're writing.

CHARACTER ONE	CHARACTER TWO	CHARACTER THREE	CHARACTER FOUR	CHARACTER FIVE
Clean Queen Bossy pants Organizational wizard Competitive	Bitter Miserly Selfish Greedy Dishonest	Geek Socially inept Stress eater	Trickster Master of self-promotion Dubious morality Lover of rum	Wary Unpredictable Spontaneous Reckless Loyal

ASSIGNMENT: Pulling from the assignment above, complete a what-could-happen list based on your character's obsession.

ASSIGNMENT: Once you've done at least one *what if* (ideally, you'd do at least ten, then choose the best option), go ahead and create the barebones of a scene where that *what if* could blossom into a funny moment in your future book. Remember my example about the older woman who'd been dropped into a young workforce environment? That's what I want you to do.

ASSIGNMENT: COMPLETE the chart below.

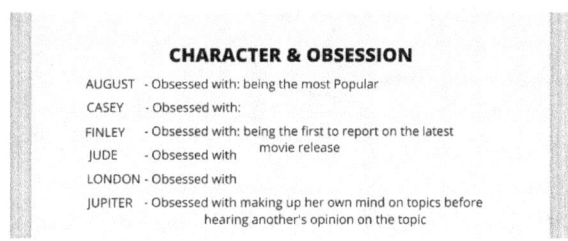

CHARACTER & OBSESSION

AUGUST - Obsessed with: being the most Popular

CASEY   - Obsessed with:

FINLEY - Obsessed with: being the first to report on the latest
JUDE   - Obsessed with   movie release

LONDON - Obsessed with

JUPITER - Obsessed with making up her own mind on topics before
            hearing another's opinion on the topic

ASSIGNMENT: Based on the characters on the list – place two of them in a fixed proximity environment (like an elevator or office or bed). Based on their obsessions, how would they react to one another? Put three of them together, how would they interact?

ASSIGNMENT: Watch your favorite sitcoms and, in the table below, make a list of each character's traits. Draw upon these traits when you're creating your own characters.

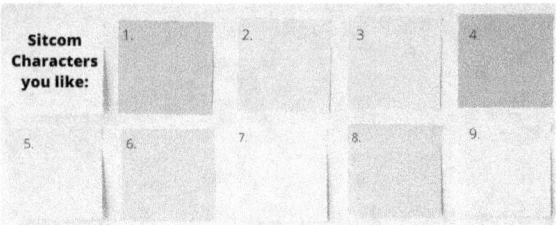

Sitcom Characters you like:	1.	2.	3	4
5.	6.	7.	8.	9.

ASSIGNMENT: Your job is to peruse the list of traits in the link provided below and pull out some additional traits you can turn into obsessions for comedic purposes during a scene in your novel: https://www.litinfocus.com/100-character-traits-list-free-printable-pdf/

ASSIGNMENT: Write a manifesto for a character in a book you're plotting. What obsessions can you pull from it that'll allow you to add humor hits to your novel?

ASSIGNMENT: Brainstorm scenes to go with these obsessions.

ASSIGNMENT: Keep a notebook with the times you felt one of the lighter negative emotions. Those are: Embarrassment. Confused. Frustrated. Later, see if you can repurpose something from your life into your novel in a funny way.

ASSIGNMENT: Create a broad-themed word list for your characters based on their stuff...like their careers or hobbies. Now, use those words to make a top ten list in the following categories:

ASSIGNMENT: Look at the premises of movies in the same genre you write. Then reimagine those premises as one of your future books.

ASSIGNMENT: Research one-liners that make you laugh.

ASSIGNMENT: Research one-liners that make your target audience laugh. You can pull these from the pages of bestsellers or movies in your genre.

Remember, what makes you laugh may not make your reader laugh. You're writing your book for the reader.

ASSIGNMENT: Use your discovered one-liners—all of them—to come up with new ones of your own. Do this by making note of any formula that's being used, then copy the formula - not the joke. Just like I did with syllogisms. NEVER THE JOKE. Don't skimp on this assignment. Find a hundred quotes and reimagine them all with the thought to make them funny.

ASSIGNMENT: Beneath each example, create your own funny line by using the one above it as a guide.

ASSIGNMENT: Go back to your one-liner assignment. Can you change several of them into understatement humor?

ASSIGNMENT: Create a simple truth humor hit for your current WIP. Do it now, while you have a sample in front of you.

ASSIGNMENT: Below, I've listed several clichés. Go ahead and twist them and include them in a book. I showed you how it's done with the first several.

*Note – Isn't **ASSIGNMENT** a weird looking word on paper?

Twenty-Five

RESOURCES

RESOURCES

RESOURCESFor those who wish to do a deep dive into how to be funny, I've listed all my resources below.

- Dave Fox Class - "Humor Writing: How to Think, Write, Speak, And Be Funnier"

- Gene Perret & Linda Perret book - *Comedy Writing Self-Taught Workbook*

- J. Timothy King Article - "1001 Character Quirks for Writing Fiction"

- Jerry Corley - "13 Major Comedy Structures - Breaking the Comedy DNA"

- John Vorhaus - "The Comic Toolbox"

- Jerry Seinfeld, Author - *The Syllogisms of Seinfeld*

- Judd Apatow Masterclass - "Developing Life Into Story"

- Kevin Heart - YouTube

- Leigh Anne Jasheway Class, "Writer's Digest Comedy Writing Workshop," and her books, *101 Comedy Games* and *Yoga For Your Funny Bone*

- Mark Shatz & Mel Helitzer Book - *Comedy Writing Secrets*

- Michael Hauge DVD - *Writing Romantic Comedies and Love Stories*

- Paul Milham book - *How To Write Comedy Characters*

- Roger Von Oech book - *A Whack on the Side of the Head*

- Scott Dikkers book - *How To Write Funny*

- Steve Martin Masterclass - "Growing As a Performer"

- Stephen Hoover - "Comedy Techniques: The Immediate Reverse"

Twenty-Six

ALSO BY LISA WELLS

Lisa Wells

Also by Lisa Wells

https://www.lisawellsauthor.com/books.html

Romantic Comedy

The Seduction of Kinley Foster

The Attraction of Adeline

Aggie the Horrible Versus Max the Pompous Ass

The Impromptu Nanny Contract (June 2022)

Paranormal Romantic Comedy (Singles Town Series)

Hexes and O's

It's a Curse Thing

Cup of Spirits

Paranormal Women's Fiction (Magical Midlife Moonlighting Series)

The Undead Life of Molly Thorn

The Magical Midlife of Molly Thorn (early spring of 2022)

The Bewitched Resolution of Molly Thorn (summer of 2022)

How to Write Books

How To Add Humor To Your Novel

How To Add Unforgettable Dialogue To Your Novel (2023)

Twenty-Seven
Chapter 27

About The Author

Lisa Wells writes romantic comedy with enough steam to fog your eyeglasses, your brain, and sometimes your Kindle screen. On the other hand, her eighty-year-old mother-in-law has read Lisa's steamiest book and lived to offer her commentary. Which went something like this: You used words I've never heard of...

She lives in Missouri with her husband and slightly-chunky rescue dog. Lisa loves dark chocolate, red wine, and those rare mornings when her skinny jeans fit. Which isn't often, considering the first two entries on her love-it list.

To learn more about all of Lisa's books, visit:

Newsletter: https://bit.ly/LisaWellsRomanceAu-thorNewsletter

Website: https://www.lisawellsauthor.com
Facebook Group — Lisa's Up All Night Readers: https://bit.ly/UpAllNightReaders

Instagram: https://www.instagram.com/lisawellsauthor/
BookBub: https://www.bookbub.com/au-thors/lisa-wells

www.ingramcontent.com/pod-product-compliance
Lightning Source LLC
Chambersburg PA
CBHW071158120626
46546CB00006B/2324